Robert Frost, October 30, 1956

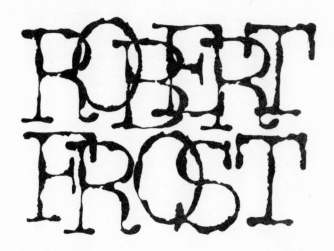

ROBERT FROST

A TIME TO TALK

CONVERSATIONS &
INDISCRETIONS
RECORDED BY

ROBERT FRANCIS

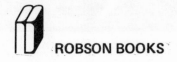

ROBSON BOOKS

FIRST PUBLISHED IN GREAT BRITAIN IN 1973 BY
ROBSON BOOKS LTD. 28 POLAND STREET,
LONDON W1V 3DB. COPYRIGHT © ROBERT FRANCIS
1972. FRONTISPIECE PHOTOGRAPH BY ROBERT
FRANCIS

ISBN 0 903895 01 3

Printed in Great Britain by Lewis Reprints Ltd. member
of Brown Knight & Truscott Group London and Tonbridge

CONVERSATIONS

1950/1959

NOBODY would have called Frost a compulsive talker. His flow was too easy, too relaxed, too seemingly inevitable for there to be any sense of strain or competition. It was just that he said such interesting things, and kept on saying them, that people around him usually kept still and listened.

Perhaps in a group of men a new book had come up for comment. One man might say it was a good book; another man, that it wasn't a good book. Then Frost's voice would be heard, not making any judgment at all, but simply quoting one sentence from that book, one salient, significant sentence. It was unprofessorial enough to be startling.

An envious person might have called Frost's talk a monologue. But it wasn't a monologue either. It had the give-and-take of true conversation. If Frost did most of the giving and the others most of the taking, their silent role was nevertheless essential. Similarly when Frost spoke from the platform, one felt that it was the audience's wordless response on which Frost depended for his next word. To leave so much to the participation of the audience and to the spur of the moment meant for both audience and speaker constant drama and surprise. It also meant for Frost himself, by his own testimony, a never-absent nervousness. To achieve spontaneity he had to take risks.

But in private when he was talking with only one or two people, he was utterly relaxed and at ease. There was still the constant surprise, but no risks, since he was not trying to sparkle or entertain. At such times Frost's talk seemed effortless and the speaker emptied of all self-consciousness.

If you ask how he could flow so endlessly, the answer is that his outflow of talk was fed by a ceaseless inflow of observation, musing, browsing, comparison-making. Whatever else he was doing or not doing, he seemed at all times to be thinking about what interested him. Unavoidable duties might now and then interrupt what he wanted to do, but they could not interrupt his flow of thought.

I have heard him speak of his "protective laziness." Perhaps it was less laziness than the freedom he demanded for himself to live his own inner life. I never knew him pressed for time. I never saw him glance at a watch or clock. For him, apparently, deadlines did not exist. And so he accumulated an enormous store of things to talk about, and everything he talked about he had thought over till it had the impress of his personality.

Generally after a conversation with Frost I felt a need to keep his talk, as far as possible, from being lost in "the stream of everything that runs away."1* So I made written records. Soon after a visit I would begin to jot down the various topics he had touched on as they occurred to me. A day or two later I would write out and enter in my journal what I remembered him saying on these topics. I almost never had any trouble in remembering what he had said, such being the vividness of his remarks. Sometimes I paraphrased or summarized; other times I could catch his very language. But in any case I believe I have been faithful to his meaning. After all, I had no other motive than to be as exact as possible. When I have quoted Frost's remarks, and those of others, I have indicated to the reader that the quotation is not necessarily letter-perfect by having the words, as I remember them, set in Italic type.

---

* These footnotes are cordially dedicated to my neighbor and fellow-poet, David R. Clark (also professor of English in the University of Massachusetts and Yeats authority), who asked for notes never guessing he would become one of them.
1. Line from "West-Running Brook."

Two days ago Robert Frost, with Armour Craig,[2] called on me on the day before he returned to Cambridge after his month in Amherst. It was the first time I had seen him this spring. It was the first time he had seen my house. He expressed approval of everything indoors and out. My wild apple tree was at the height of bloom and loaded. Looking at it from indoors, he said the sticks of the window improved the tree—that was what art did. Outdoors he said the fringed polygala[3] was trying to be not a bird but an airplane. Later observation on my part confirmed the felicity of the comparison.

We discussed again Mark 4:1–12, to which he refers in his poem, "Directive." At first he maintained that Jesus had said it and meant it, and that he (Frost) agreed. Namely, not merely the fact that some people were for one reason or another excluded, but that they needed to be and ought to be excluded. Later he said with a twinkle: *I know why I brought that into the poem. I wanted to say that it was as good a passage as any other that people wish were not in the Bible.* I said, *Ah, that is a good reason. That is the sort of reason I would expect of you.*

Personalities: James Still,[4] James Hayford,[5] Wade Van Dore,[6] Sidney Robins.[7] I wish I could remember what he said about me. *You*

2. George Armour Craig, professor of English in Amherst College.

3. Fringed polygala, *Polygala paucifolia* of the milkwort family, a small wild flower with pink blossoms, the two lateral sepals wing-shaped and the three petals joined together to form a tube. Found on the bank just west of my house.

4. James Still, Kentucky poet and writer of fiction.

5. James Hayford, Vermont poet, who received at his graduation from Amherst College in 1935 a fellowship from Robert Frost, nicknamed "The Desert Fellowship."

6. Wade Van Dore, poet and protégé of Frost, having been at one time, in his own words, Frost's "hired man."

7. Sidney Robins, alternately professor of philosophy and Unitarian clergyman. Pastor in Amherst at this time.

are one of the few people I know who does (settle down to write consistently and persistently, settle down to face life?).

Yesterday evening as I sat reading, a car drove into the yard and up to the house, its headlights making a sudden exterior illumination. It was Charles Green[8] bringing Robert Frost; or more accurately, Robert Frost bringing Charles Green.

Frost came up to the door mumbling something about civil liberties[9] (much as in May he entered to the password of "the running milkman").[10]

He said if he had known I had a telephone, he might have made me come to see *him*.

He began by telling of two callers he had had that day. One a Greek boy teaching at Harvard, who was at outs with everybody and wanted to get away from it all, but didn't seem able to. The other a young Amherst student from Boston, whose poetry was so smooth and slippery you couldn't get hold of anything to comment about.

He spoke of other people who wanted (but not enough) to live independently and with leisure. (The implication being that I do.) A person who in a theater fire stands aside from the rush, preferring to get burned than mashed, but often escaping both fates by discovering a little exit of his own.

8. Charles R. Green, librarian of the Jones Library, Amherst, founder and curator there of a notable Frost collection, and co-compiler of the Frost bibliography.
9. I was active in the Hampshire County chapter of the American Civil Liberties Union.
10. "The Running Milkman," title of one of 150 "familiar" essays of mine on the Home Forum Page of the *C.S. Monitor* from 1938 to 1954.

Frost said he had never lifted his finger to advance his career, but that everything had come to him. He spoke of once thinking of sending a poem to William D. Howells, but deciding to wait till it was in print and so letting it make that much better impression. It was Howells who finally asked Frost to call, gave him a little book of his own eclogues as if to say, "See, I've been doing them too, but with less notice than you are receiving."

As an illustration of his laissez-faire and also of an acquired shrewdness, he told of once selling a horse to a good-hearted but astute business man who thought Frost had paid $200 and so offered him $150. Frost had actually paid only $75 and so made $75. He was sick in bed and pretty much down and out at the time, but he was beginning to believe that he was as bright as the next man.

He dwelt on his early timidity. When his mother died, he was not bold enough to go on with the school they kept together, for though he could face the pupils he could not face their parents.

The farm his grandfather bought for him (to retire to and die on) cost $1700. Frost sold it ten years later for $1900. He had paid an annual $30 in taxes. So he figured he had enjoyed the place for an annual rent of $10. He went to England with his family (six in all) and lived there three years and came home, all for $3600.

When reporters ask him why he writes poetry, he may give any one of these answers:

To see if I can make my poems all different.

Having got into a poem, to see if I can get out.

To do something women have never succeeded in doing—write eclogues.

At his reading Friday, Frost remarked that he had just noticed that the portrait of his first sponsor, William Hayes Ward,[11] was hanging

11. William Hayes Ward, editor-in-chief from 1896 to 1913 of *The Independent*, in which several of Frost's poems were published.

———

on the rear wall facing him. All the years Frost had been returning to Johnson Chapel, the portrait had been there, but never noticed before.

Ward had turned against Frost when the latter left college. Other enemies. John Crowe Ransom, a book of whose poems Frost had read for a publisher many years ago and recommended. Yvor Winters who used to send poems to him. But Frost was too honest to pretend that he liked them. Now Winters *honestly* finds everything about Frost wrong.

O'Donnell[12] is trying to make him orthodox, and is despairing of the state of the world. *Not Christian attitude*, F. remarked. *We can at least bet on ourselves*, F. says he told him. Mrs. Whicher[13] he respects in spite of her being so Episcopalian. *Cocktailianism-Episcopalianism*. Funny thing, highest-marked boy to go through Amherst was Brower;[14] ideal student at Barnard was Harriet Fox.

Lee was a bright boy. Grant fiftieth in his class, but Grant was greater general. Good man, never told a dirty story, acknowledged and corrected his own mistakes. Never overestimated enemy's strength as MacArthur does. Common man but great. Truman common man but ordinary.

Donald Adams,[15] friend, sensitive, shy, poor speaker, nice face, family trouble.

Frost and Green consented to drink a cup of postum with me. My

12. William G. O'Donnell, professor of English in the University of Massachusetts, and close student of Frost's poetry.
13. Harriet Fox Whicher, professor of English in Mount Holyoke College, and wife of George Frisbie Whicher, professor of English in Amherst College.
14. Reuben Brower became professor of English at Harvard in 1953, and master of Adams House in 1954. Previously he had taught English and Greek in Amherst College.
15. J. Donald Adams, well-known editor of page 2 of the *New York Times Sunday Book Review*.

fire was more successful than the one Frost remembered in May. He had me demonstrate a Nantucket Knot[16] for Green.

He asked my address. *Simpler than you would believe*, I told him. *R. Francis, Amherst, Mass.*

He asked about my new small book of poems[17] (which I had sent him). I said that a little over half the edition sold had brought in enough money to pay the printer; the rest of the edition would keep me in print for years to come.

He said his amusingly rhymed Christmas poem.[18] I asked when we were to see his new Columbus poem in print.[19] He promised to send me a manuscript copy. In return I promised to send him my recent "Two Lords"[20] which I had read aloud at mention of Episcopal cocktails.

16. Nantucket Knot, ten full sheets of newspaper rolled into a long tube and tied in a double knot. Serves a sulking fireplace fire by providing long-burning kindling and by holding up logs for circulation of air.

17. *The Face Against the Glass*, my small paper-covered book of poems privately published in 1950. My previous three poetry volumes had all been brought out by Macmillan.

18. "Our Doom to Bloom" (*In the Clearing*).

19. A poem first called "For Columbus Day," and later entitled "America Is Hard to See" (*In the Clearing*).

20. A poem of mine still unpublished.

THE TWO LORDS OF AMHERST

The two Lords, Jeffery and Jehovah, side by side
Proclaim that hospitality lives and Jesus died.

Jeffery in white-washed brick, Jehovah in gray stone,
Both testify man does not live by bread alone.

From sacred love to bed and board and love profane
One could dart back and forth and not get wet in rain.

How providentially inclusive the design:
Here are the cocktails, here the sacramental wine.

———

They left about 10:45. We turned flashlight and headlights on the "eolith palladium"[21] in the "grove." Frost asked about my stone step, and I told them the story involving Chester Woodard.[22] *He is a man as New England as you are*, I told him. *More so, for he is nothing else.*

SEPTEMBER 13, 1951

Robert Frost sat in this room on the evening of December 10, 1950, as I have already told, and remarked that he had never lifted a finger to advance his career. That is a glorious thing for great rewards to come to a man unsought. It also can be a glorious thing to be an earnest and passionate seeker. I am doing far, far more than lifting a finger to advance my career, yet am doing it in such a way that no one may know I am lifting a finger.

> Here is the holy, here the not-so-holy host.
> Here are the potted palms and here the Holy Ghost.
>
> Tell, if you can and will, which is more richly blest:
> The guest Jehovah entertains or Jeffery's guest.

21. "Eolith palladium," a phrase in Frost's poem, "Of the Stones of the Place." "Eolith,"—"A chipped flint, shaped probably by natural agencies, thought to have been used as an implement by early man." "Palladium,"—"A statue of Pallas Athene, especially one in the citadel of Troy on which the safety of the city was supposed to depend. A safe-guard." Both definitions from the *Random House Dictionary of the English Language*.
22. Chester Woodard, Leverett builder and contractor, who in 1940 built my house, Fort Juniper. The story of the stone doorstep is told in my autobiography, *The Trouble With Francis* (University of Massachusetts Press, 1971), p. 68.

Two afternoons ago I spent an hour with Robert Frost in his room at the Lord Jeff.[23] America's greatest living poet, the most successful, recognized, honored, sat in undramatic fashion and chatted with one whom he himself called "the best neglected poet." I am the poet whom the editors reject; Frost is the poet who rejects the editors. He had declined to contribute to *Poetry*'s current Fortieth Anniversary Number. He said he had told Shapiro he would *give* him a poem sometime.

I took with me a manuscript copy of *With The Year's Cooling*.[24] *Have you written a book?* he asked. *Only poems,* I said. I spoke of much revision, not only of the new but of some of the old. Frost shook his head, so to speak. I hadn't thought at the moment that I had been violating one of his pet theories: that a poem not only should but *must* be written in a single free-flowing run. Frost likened the process to Benvenuto Cellini's casting the statue of Perseus: it had to be done all at once. I suggested that he, Frost, wrote his poems with the speed of working of a water colorist; whereas I worked and reworked mine like an oil painter. I hadn't meant to flatter myself. Question from Frost: Why were all the greatest paintings oils?

He took a hard crack at Yeats as an extreme revisionist. Yeats who had chewed pencils and sweated blood till the time came (for a time) he wrote no more poetry. But Frost was equally hard on his sexiness, both personal and poetic.

Abbott at Buffalo[25] who has the collection of "worksheets of

23. The Lord Jeffery Inn, Amherst's leading hostelry located next to Grace Episcopal Church and near Amherst College.
24. Tentative title of my then current collection of poems for publication, which became ultimately *The Orb Weaver* (Wesleyan University Press, 1960).
25. Charles D. Abbott, librarian of the Lockwood Memorial Library of the University of Buffalo, and founder and director of its collection of materials in contemporary poetry.

poems" he called a fool. Forty versions of a poem by Auden. As if a poem's value were to be measured by the trouble it cost. He himself took pains to hide the few changes he had made in his own poems. He said people always resented his changes, and yet overvalued them, sometimes when they were mere accidents of copying. Once he wrote out one of his poems for a woman, with some variations from the printed version. Later she told him she had lost the holograph when her house burned down. Frost asked her if she knew who had set the fire.

Speaking of women, he touched on Mrs. Adlai Stevenson, who is heading *Poetry*'s fund-raising campaign. *You know she writes poetry, just as her former husband is literary too. I wonder what the trouble was between them, whether he didn't like her poetry or she his.* Another poetess: Mrs. Francis Biddle (Chapin). Loves Washington society, yet wants to be a poet. Frost repeated to me what she had told him that St. John Perse had once said to her. *Madame, in your busy life you have time for prose, but not for poetry.*

A single fly in the room was pestering Frost. While waiting for it to light on him once again, the great man explained how he usually could kill such a pest. Poising his leonine head in concentration and lifting a ponderous hand, he brought it down with a resounding smack. Then he glanced at me a bit sheepishly. *I didn't get it, did I?*

He tried again, without success. Finally the fly came over to me. *It's all right, Mr. Frost*, I said, *it's over here now.*

But the fly returned to him again. And again he tried to swat it. *You're making a principle of it*, I cautioned. *A point of honor.*

At another point in the conversation Frost likened the typical current poet to a mosquito coming around with that thin whine, looking for a reader in whom to sink his proboscis, but finding only green foliage available. *They don't know how much their pessimism is due to failure to get published.*

Johnson dismissed Milton's early poems as mere preparation for

Paradise Lost, whereas (according to Frost) they were the real thing and the epic was only "grand." In *Samson* Milton broke away from his rhetoric and did something great again.

Browning: wrote some good poems and some not so good.

Vachel Lindsay: didn't know when he had done well and when he hadn't. Kept everything as if all was on one level of value.

Fortieth Anniversary Number of *Poetry*. He held it up. *Here are all the names. But if anyone was going to feel envious of anything here———*

Richard Wilbur. *One of the best.* But Harvard is making too much of him for his own good. Advanced him rapidly. Honorary degree from Amherst. Are they getting ready to bring him back here? Goes in very smart circle, Harry Levin's.

James Hayford. Frost spoke more appreciatively of him than he did last winter at Converse Library. Half-admires his seriousness in settling down to poetry as his main pursuit, but wishes his poems were not all "snippets."

How was I going to get home? I said I would walk. *You're the darnedest*, he exclaimed not without a touch of approval. *And you're good-natured about it all. I know that. Not pessimistic. Not optimistic. Good-natured.*

I left the manuscript with him. *Please forget about the revisions*, I asked. *All right*, he said. *I'll remember Gray who took eighteen years to write his Elegy.*

OCTOBER 26, 1952

I was outdoors washing windows about three o'clock Thursday afternoon, the twenty-third, when a car drew in off the road. Wishing to

---

13

finish the window I was working on, I did not look to see who it was. In a few moments the car drove away, but someone was coming toward the house. I started down to meet him. It was Robert Frost.

Before going in, we strolled about for a few minutes. He wanted to know where my boundary line ran, remarked on the variety of my trees, and asked if I had been troubled with the white pine weevil. When he saw that some of my pines had been attacked and that I had removed only the vertical shoot, he advised that I take off four of the whorl of five shoots just below to leave a single leader and insure a single-trunk tree. Did I know that the white pine, our finest tree, had been one cause of the American Revolution, since the colonists resented the king's claim to all the best pines for masts for his ships?

A dead female mantis, which I had found that morning, lay on a chair. Frost surprised me by the interest he took in the insect. He asked no end of questions—what they ate, how they wintered, etc. Hearing of their cannibalism, he told me I was fond of them because they showed so vividly what it was in nature I didn't like. I said my attitude was somewhat ambivalent: I gave them every care and consideration, but I stopped at supplying them with food. They had to forage for themselves.

As we started in, Frost noticed my house needed painting and said so. He was surprised to hear it had been painted twice in its twelve years. He said he had often thought of building himself but never had, though an addition he had put on his house in Vermont was about the size of my house.

We looked at my collection of mantis shells, egg-cases, and mantis mummies. It was with a reference to the mantids that he began to discuss my poems. *They are like your interest in the mantis: there are always two things there.* He started to say, *Where will you find any*——— but checked himself with the remark that he would not compare me to anybody else, but that my poems were good. *I like them for so many different reasons. And always have.* He said I was a philosopher, and referred to some sort of "indignation" in my poetry. I have forgotten the qualifying word. Said my satire had sting. Mentioned "The Two Lords of Amherst" and "Picasso and Matisse"[26] by title.

As to why the editors rejected me so often, Frost professed not to know, then tried to guess. Was it because the poems were too lean, too tight, too dry for them? Did the editors want more juice? Did they fail to feel the emotion in my paradoxes (which Frost felt that I felt)? Did I possibly repeat the good-evil paradox too often? If these were the reasons, there really wasn't much I could do about it.

He told me about a neighbor of his in Ripton who writes for the Saturday Evening Post a certain type of story about a "tractor man." Frost said he had read only one and hadn't found it very funny. Had been told all of them were on the same model. Well, this writer got his start in a strange way. As a freshman at Cornell (I think) he had handed in a story and got a *D* for it. Years later, feeling a lingering fondness for the thing, he sent it to the *SEP*. They wrote that they liked it but that it would need certain changes. But the next he knew they had printed it and sent him a big check. *Which goes to show?* Frost asked him. *That nobody knows nothing about it*, came the answer.

I said I had hoped he would tell me which poems to throw out. Oh, if that was what I wanted, he said, he might keep the poems longer, say till his return in spring. (When he left, he took the manuscript volume with him.)

My effort to make a living from my writing he contrasted with his own avoidance of putting too much financial trust in his poetry. From not having expected to make money on poetry, he came in time to make a considerable part of his income from it. But he was

26. "Picasso and Matisse" is included in *New Poems by American Poets* (Ballantine Books, 1953).

15

not suggesting any change in my policy. If I could do it, all right. There had been some talk, years ago, of a book of prose from him. People still occasionally asked him about it. He smiled at me. As for his poems, his publishers had told him at the outset that he should have a new book every few years. It has worked out about one every seven years.

He talked for some time about his luck. He had been lucky in the early years to be published just enough, yet not too much, so that his first book came with a sort of freshness and surprise. For a long time he had never even thought of a volume, supposing that a poet needed to have much more response from magazines before he could interest a publisher. His putting together the first volume had been a sort of casual play as he sat on the floor with thirty or so of the poems spread out around him.

He had been lucky with his first publisher too, David Nutt. (*A woman dressed all in black, as if she had just risen from the sea, came into the office and said: 'I will speak for Mr. Nutt.'*) He had been innocent about the book, just as he had been innocent for years about traveling with a dog, supposing that the dog had to go unhappily in the baggage car, when actually, at no greater total expense, he could have taken the dog with him in a room in a sleeping car.

He owed something to Pound, who liked to promote new writers, but didn't like them to surpass him later on. Pound might have been troublesome if Frost had kept too close to him. He had never broken with Pound, just drifted away. He also owed something to John Gound Fletcher, another American in England at the time, who had put out several small books of poems in the same year as Frost's first publication, and whose overaggressiveness reflected favorably on Frost.

His career had been hard on his children. They had not wanted to profit by his fame, and he had tried not to get in their way. But there had been jealousy involved, unexpressed jealousy. Roosevelt's children had had the same problem in more exaggerated form, but whereas R.'s children had been pushed too much into prominence, F.'s had been pushed too much in the background.

His granddaughter from Billings, Montana, is now a freshman at Smith. (Her mother, Marjorie Frost Fraser, died shortly after childbirth.) Very nice girl, but very Western. Expected he would come over to Smith and read his poems informally, and was not prepared to hear him say he couldn't do that, though he would come over and sit with the girls some evening. Her father,[27] a liberal Democrat, is running for Congress. He has been *a very perfect father to her* and his mother *a very perfect grandmother*.

Frost said he had decided that very morning to put off his annual reading and talk until spring. But he was meeting informally with several college groups. He had told Bill Gibson[28] that at one of them he thought he would talk on Poe. *Oh, yes*, said Bill, *I believe there is something of a Poe revival. Wilbur is doing something at Harvard.* As if, Frost commented, he had chosen Poe because of a revival. Better reason for not choosing Poe. *They're all so up-to-the-minute. And cliquy.*

He had had a visit with Leland Nichols, local piano teacher, who when Frost came to Amherst had been one of four boys who cultivated the arts and burnt incense to a statue of Buddha.

Henry Seidel Canby used to want Frost to write more like Milton. He praised the line: "But still unstoried, artless, unenhanced." Why couldn't he write more lines like that? Some jealousy was involved, Canby having been a prime champion of S. V. Benét.

Though a friend, he called Douglas Southall Freeman, biographer of Poe as well as of Washington, *A pompous, self-important man,*

27. Willard E. Fraser.
28. Walker Gibson, poet and professor of English in Amherst College, later at New York University, at present at the University of Massachusetts. A neighbor, then and now, on Market Hill Road.

and a bad historian. Oh, he writes pretty good history. But he would write better if he got more sleep.

By now Charles Green, who had brought Frost out and then gone on to LeClair's[29] to see about some upholstering, had returned and joined the conversation over coffee and postum (postum for F.). Both men had testified they needed precisely eight hours sleep at night. Frost was scornful of Freeman's, or anybody else's, overestimation of the value of time. *As the English say of us* terrible *Americans: 'May I have five minutes of your* valuable *time?'* He looked as if he were dislocating his jaw in getting out the word.

Frost and Green exchanged reminiscences of their experiences with goats. Frost also spoke of bees. Hesitated to have them in Vermont because of fear of bears. He told of raising dwarf watermelons this past summer. The watermelon was God's riddle. (*Not his only one*, I interposed.) Of three that look equally promising, one will be under-ripe, one over-ripe, and one just right.

It seemed to me Frost was more appreciative of Green than he used to be. But at one point he twitted him a bit.

F: Are you still trying to get rid of those bibliographies?
G: Actually, I'm trying to hold onto some.
F: How many do you have?
G: Just a few.
F: That's what you said ten years ago. Come, tell the truth.
G: I *am* telling the truth.

On leaving, Frost admired the big stone doorstep, the sweet-briar bush nearby (wondered if he could get one for his place), the poverty grass (the name of which he asked),[30] and my strawberry bed.

---

29. Ernest LeClair, furniture repairer and upholsterer with shop on Market Hill Road.
30. Poverty grass, *Andropogon scoparius*.

18

As we went out the door, I had asked him if he actually recommended my having a goat. He said he did. But then he wondered about pasturage. I didn't want a goat eating up all my bushes and small trees. He too, like me, liked to let things grow as they pleased, come as they would. That letting things come came close to his whole philosophy, I suggested. Yes, he said, he let the world come as it would, only giving it now and then "a kick and a touch." It was like steering a car: you kept your hands on the steering wheel, but lightly.[31] I remarked that whether or not you could do that depended somewhat on the condition of the car.

Green handed me a little paper book of matches with Eisenhower's picture on it. I thanked him and said I would use it but not publicly. At that, the two of them, good-naturedly, lit into me. Frost said: *There are two games—checkers and give-away. We have been giving away to Germany, to Japan, to China, etc. etc. etc. I want checkers for a change.*

OCTOBER 29, 1952

When Frost praises my poems highly, am I wise to accept his praise unqualifiedly? Am I wise to assume that he is right and that all the people who do not praise me are wrong? In commenting on *With The Year's Cooling*, he gave not the slightest hint of any new power in my recent work. He liked the poems, yes, but he added that he always had. When I spoke of my determination to do better work, he spoke of a poet's normal development, not from poorer work to better, but from work expressive of one age to work expressive of a later age.

31. See pp. 92–95 in this book.

Frost asked me what I did when I was not writing. How much that question reveals—of the man who asked it and of his slight acquaintance, after all, with the man he asked it of.

He said he spent considerable time keeping his cutter-bar in repair. It was a necessary job and at the same time a sort of play for him. He seemed to assume that a man in my position would need something like that, something to take up his time and take up his mind when not engaged on intellectual and artistic labor.

I told him I read, wrote letters, did some gardening, and took care of my house. I could have added to the list. What I did not tell him was that the day is never long enough, or half long enough, for me. His own experience has been so different from mine that he might not have been able to believe me. In any case he could not have avoided some scorn for so "busy" a person.

You can't lie on your back, he said, and then repeated, as a sort of generalization. As if the avoidance of lying on my back were any problem to me!

APRIL 21, 1954

In the afternoon Hyde Cox[32] brought Robert Frost out to call. It was so warm that we sat outdoors—in my three old weathered chairs. Mr. Frost wore a light-weight gray suit; his shirt was open at the throat. Cox and I were in our shirt-sleeves.

As we sat down Frost seemed buried within himself and reluctant

32. Hyde Cox, of Crow Island, Manchester, Mass. See p. 80 in this book.

to make the effort to come out. But after a few moments he emerged into his familiar self and kept up a lively flow of conversation for two hours.

He mentioned the visit he had had that morning from O'D.[33] and E.[34] regarding his part in the "New England Anthology."[35] To get him talking on the subject of freedom (the theme of the series), they had asked him if rhyme and meter did not restrict a poet's freedom of utterance. He had said to them that a poet had to start with two major restrictions anyway—language (the dictionary) and grammar; and that having successfully "taken on" those two, a poet should be in the mood to take on something more.

F. complained that so many poets today are satisfied with poetry as texture. Their poems are like the pieces of cloth hung up instead of pictures in some arty houses. His advice to such poets is to make something out of their cloth. *Make a pair of pants.*

Nothing he said all afternoon was more interesting than his account of writing his first poem when a sophomore in Lawrence High School. Nobody had told him how to write a poem. Nobody had told him anything. He just began. He was on his way home one dusty March afternoon, his books in a strap, when he began to compose some ballad-like verses on the *Tristes Noches* of Cortez. After getting home, he kept working away until he had finished the story and included the names of all the relevant people. This poem was accepted by the senior editor of the high school literary paper and published.

The first poem F. ever sent out to a national magazine was also published. This was a couple of years later, the magazine was *The*

33. William O'Donnell, see note 12.
34. Frederick C. Ellert, now professor emeritus of German and former head of the German and Russian Department in the University of Massachusetts.
35. *New England Anthology*, a series of ten tapes of readings by poets with New England affiliations, made in 1954, under a grant from the Ford Foundation, for broadcast over educational radio.

Independent, and the poem was "My Butterfly." For it he received $20. *Not so bad*, he reckoned. *Twenty dollars a week?* But it was twenty *years* before he was earning anything like twenty dollars a week from his poetry.

We got to talking about American birds that had become extinct or nearly extinct. "Down to ten copies," as F. put it, before anybody did anything to stop the decline. He told of a man who after retiring devoted himself to the recovery of a certain species of bird. I mentioned eagles and that started both F. and Cox with stories. F. had seen an eagle's nest in Florida this past winter—a huge affair twenty feet thick, having been added to year after year. He had seen one young eagle peering down over the edge.

Eagles led to comments on American foreign policy. F. denounced those men in our country who were trying to get us involved in the Indo-Chinese war. He called a war between Christians and Asiatics the cruelest kind of war, for the Asiatics have far different ideas from ours on the treatment of prisoners. A son of his, he said, he would rather have shot than fall into enemy hands.

Cox related that in the annual Patriots' Day Marathon at Boston (two days ago) a Japanese boy whose name was Hiroshima and who came from Nagasaki had placed fourth. The first six places were taken by runners from "downtrodden countries" as F. put it. The American who won seventh place was excused by the newspapers for not doing better because he was a student and had to study.

Of course the two recent birthday dinners came up for comment. F. quoted the Twenty-third Psalm sardonically to hint at his attitude toward the affairs. "Thou spreadest a table before me in the presence of mine enemies."

It was not quite clear (to me, anyway) whether his "enemies" were all outside the dining room. Evidently he had not had entire say by any means as to who should be invited to the Amherst dinner. And as for the N.Y. dinner he seems not to have had any say at all.

He was surprised, he said, that Judge Medina (a man of the old school, a scholar) was there to make a speech, since F. had never met him before and had not known much about him. Two men at the N.Y. dinner threatened to mar the affair by getting objectionably drunk. One of them had talked rather insultingly to Mrs. Adlai Stevenson, who had come from Chicago for the occasion. The tone at the Amherst dinner was exceptionally good, he thought, except for President and Mrs. Chalmers[36] who never want to share F. with anyone else and who just couldn't be "handsome" about it.

I said I had been trying to explain to my friends how it happened that I went to his birthday dinner and didn't even speak to him.

But I bowed to you, said F. *Did you see me?*

Yes, I said. *But I wasn't sure you weren't bowing to May Sarton who sat beside me.*

This led to considerable comment—mostly favorable—about Miss Sarton—the quality of her writing as well as her more personal charms.

She writes better prose than verse, was F.'s concluding judgment.

The talk having touched on Thornton Wilder, Cox exclaimed, *Do you realize how he* began *his speech?—'Poetry is a plummet that goes deep!'* He and I said the words in chorus and enacted the Wilder gesture, an upward and downward plunge of the forefinger.

Thornton's a good boy, said F. mildly.

At the mention of President Cole's speech, I said I thought his conclusion had not been altogether happy.

What did he say? asked F.

Why, he said that radioactive ashes go halfway round the earth and fall on Amherst, but that you *go all the way round.*

But he said some good things too, said Cox.

---

36. Gordon Keith Chalmers, president of Kenyon College, and Mrs. Chalmers, the poet and former Roberta Teale Swartz.

Yes, said I. *That 'legend' story, he told that well. The more I think about it the more meaning I find in it.*

Then Mr. Frost told us what had actually happened. It was back in 1927 or 1926. For the final examination in his course he had written on the board: *Do something appropriate to this course that you think would please me.* He told the class that he would be upstairs, if anybody needed to ask a question. He had given each student three blue books, and some of them filled all three. Having tried to please him that way, some of them came upstairs afterwards to assure him how they had enjoyed the course and how much it had meant to them. (One boy who merely signed his name to the blue book and went home got the only *A*.)

When I tell that story now, said F., *people say: ' Of course* you *could do that, Mr. Frost.' Old-maid teachers*—and he mimicked their half-disapproving smile. *But they could do a thing like that just as well as I did. After all, at that time I wasn't anybody much.*

When I spoke of hoping to have a closer look sometime at the Wyeth painting[37] that was presented to F. at the dinner (by Cox), they said I should see the other Wyeth[38] that Charles Morgan[39] had loaned to F. for his Amherst stay. So great a painting it was that F. wondered how Morgan had let it out of his hands. He wouldn't mind owning it himself. *Tell him*, he said to Cox, *that he couldn't put it in safer hands.*

Of book collectors F. said they talked as if he wrote exclusively for them. Over long-distance: *Robert, surely you have something new for me.*

37. "The title of the Wyeth watercolor was simply 'Interior of a Barn in Winter.' It was painted in Chadds Ford soon after the well-known tempera painting 'The Cooling Shed.'"—Hyde Cox in a letter to me.
38. "Wind from the Sea" by Andrew Wyeth.
39. Charles H. Morgan, professor of fine arts in Amherst College and head of the department.

Funny little man, isn't he? F. said of Charles Green. I told how Green had offered me some months ago two copies of one of my books he happened to have on hand, fresh copies which he offered me at the price he had paid for them. Month after month, whenever I went to the Jones Library, he would ask me if I didn't want to take them. Since I was always walking and had plenty of other things to carry, I always thanked him and asked if I couldn't take them some time later. Finally, he put them into my hands and declined to take anything for them.

I also told of Green's distress at the temporary loss of one folder in his Frost Collection. (It contained information about the little book *Twilight* printed when F. was nineteen and containing only five poems. Of the two copies, one was destroyed and the other given to Mrs. F.) Green had told me that he had gone to sleep night after night murmuring to himself, "Twilight, twilight, twilight." Finally the lost was found.

I didn't know he was that much fool, said F.

In referring to the booklet I was touching on a sensitive spot, as I discovered. After Mrs. F.'s death, the little book was given to a collector friend who promised to keep it always. For some strange reason he sold it at auction (with other things) some years later. Now F. wants to get the book into his own hands, and can't. He is admittedly embarrassed by the episode.

In reply to his question about my own next book, I said I might try my old publishers, Macmillan, again. That led F. to say how shabbily they had treated Vachel Lindsay, persuading him at a time when he needed money to sell a manuscript for a lump sum and waive royalties. And Lindsay had been the sort of man who needed protection— from publishers as well as from other people. Whenever he did have money, he spent it with open hand, as in large tips. *The American people gave me my money and I want to return it to them.* (F. quoted him as saying this.)

As for F.'s own publishers, he said they had been exemplary toward him. They had fought among themselves—palace revolutions —blood flowing under the doors—but to him they had been only tenderly solicitous. They had never hurried him. They had "nursed him along." Old Alfred Harcourt had taken that attitude from the first, and the others had followed suit.

F. told of visiting recently the new Chicago home of *Poetry*, a Lake-Shore mansion given by Mrs. Adlai Stevenson, with art gallery and bar to boot. I asked him if it wasn't Karl Shapiro whom he had referred to anonymously at the Amherst dinner as the editor who had announced that country poetry was finished and only "city, coterie, and satiric poetry" had any standing now—and then had turned around and asked F. for some of his. F. said Shapiro had given a talk somewhere at the time of F.'s visit, and had obviously prepared his address before he knew F. was to be in the audience. With F. almost in touching distance of him, he had seemed a bit embarrassed by what he was saying. But he had gone ahead and said it. He had also said that the great subject for American poetry was and would continue to be the unhappiness of America. *Shapiro is a sociologist,* concluded F.

Poetry, like a joke, ought not to have to be explained. Whatever satisfaction he got from the *New Yorker*, he said, was dependent on how successful he was in getting the jokes. He told of a party at which Irwin Edman came up to him three times in succession, saying each time for those around him to hear: *I tell Robert, good fences make good burglars.* Each time F. tried to brush him off, and it was only when it was too late that he caught on and felt like kicking himself.

And now, I said, *you sit looking at me to see if I catch on. But don't be too disappointed in me: I'm always slow to see a joke.*

Since the two men seemed to be expecting me to make an effort, I asked if it didn't mean that only a good fence could bring out the best in a burglar.

No, said F., *that isn't it. But you wouldn't know. You don't know about crime.*

So the conversation passed from one topic to another, and it is impossible now to recall how it got where it did.

F. related to us how he had once been made president of the P.E.N. Club. However, he refused to preside at their dinner and took a seat off to one side. Henry Canby, who presided in his stead, began his remarks by saying: *Your president sits over there in the corner.* F.'s presidency seemed to peter out or lapse. Nobody told him when he ceased to be president. He said it looked to him as if he had been fired without notice.

Something made me quote Archibald MacLeish's remark when he was presented with a large award a couple of years ago. (I read it somewhere.[40]) "Now I'll have to run like a rabbit." F. wanted to know why he had said that. I answered that I supposed he had meant that having devoted so much of his life to other careers, he would have to run like a rabbit to get where he wanted to get.

Oh, the rabbit-and-turtle, said F.

And who's the turtle? I asked.

Maybe Richard Wilbur, F. chuckled. *No, not Wilbur, Carl Sandburg.* And he looked as if he had really got the right man.

The new poem that F. read at the dinner, the one about the stray dog,[41] I learned was on F.'s Christmas card this year. But the task of sending out 450 of them with usually a personal word added had proved too great. The cards were still in Cambridge, most of them. They might get sent out by July 4 as had been the case last year. I

---

40. "From here on," MacLeish told a reporter after winning the National Book Award, "I've got to run like a rabbit." This quotation is itself a quotation from an essay, "The Poetry of Archibald MacLeish," by John Ciardi in *The Atlantic Monthly* for May 1953.

41. A poem entitled "One More Brevity" from *In the Clearing*.

told him that I was keeping a little collection of his cards and that on most of them he had written a word of greeting.

That morning I had had a visit from seven-year-old Susan Gibson.[42] I repeated some of the things she had said. *Vaguely I remember that. I remember vaguely.* And: *Susan, did you see that with your own eyes or did you read it?—I saw it with my own eyes* and *I read it.* This reminded the two men that on their way out here they had seen a little fair-haired boy of four or five marching off somewhere all by himself. *Just like Blake,* said F.

Twice during our visit we glanced up as a butterfly (a Camberwell Beauty) fluttered high overhead.

But the first thing F. glanced up to see was my sun deck. He wanted to know what it was. He appreciated that when I was up there I wouldn't be able to hear my phone. Living in the country, he said, had been his own salvation from too much phone bother.

He spoke about my walking. *You'll live longer and die happier.— Do you walk right off or do you stroll?* He said his father had been an expert walker, had once taken part in a six-day walk against a famous walker. In those days walking was a recognized sport and there were professional walkers. A long walk was likely to break up because of disputes over technicalities. F. spoke of the nuisance of cars to the walker. I said that for me in Amherst cars weren't much of a problem. I tried to ignore them utterly on the road, though I was glad and thankful always to get a lift.

Wealthy Hyde Cox who had come in a brand-new fancy car (gray outside, rich red leather inside) changed the subject from automobiles to airplanes. Having read my poem about "The Buzz Plane," he said he agreed with me entirely. He would shoot the damned things if he could. I confessed that my own attitude toward planes, especially small ones, had changed somewhat since

42. Susan Gibson, daughter of Walker and Nancy Gibson.

Francis Wysocki[43] had reconnoitered my house from the air last January.

In leaving, the two men walked with me round the little path I made on my premises last summer. F. commented on my series of compost piles, said he had recently visited Louis Bromfield whose compost heaps were tremendous. He glanced at my stone god,[44] noted my strawberries, and asked about my boundaries, saying it was too bad I hadn't been able to buy more land. At the door he asked Cox about the birch feeders; and indoors, when shown my case of mantis mummies and shells, asked a little surprisingly if they were alive.

Walking down the path toward the car, he paused and picked up a stone. Very deliberately he drew back his arm, and then summoning all his strength, hurled the stone across the road. As if to say, as if to say, that even if he was eighty———

NOVEMBER 1, 1954

You write on subjects, said Wallace Stevens to Frost when they met in Key West nearly twenty years ago. *And you*, retorted Frost with equal scorn, *you write bric-a-brac*.

So the two classmates (Harvard, 1901) became friends. Friends enough for Stevens to send Frost his books as they came out. "Some more bric-a-brac" was the inscription on the latest.

This I learned a couple of weeks ago (October 12) when I was in-

43. Francis Wysocki, Amherst man living a mile or two to the south of me, who had attended a small gathering in my home to hear the Catholic anarchist, Ammon Hennacy, tell the story of his life as urgently as the Ancient Mariner, on a certain arctic afternoon before a blazing fire.
44. My "stone god" was the "eolith palladium." See note 21.

vited up to the Gibsons with whom Frost and three students were spending the evening. Frost told how, at his twenty-fifth reunion in 1926, he had told his classmates that he was not their poet, having been with them only two years. Wallace Stevens was the man. But at that time they knew of Stevens only as an insurance lawyer.

At Key West Stevens had come to call with an associate lawyer from the South, both men well along in their cups. *Frosh never fay-shed life,* said Stevens to the southerner. *Tell him the story about the woman with the wooden leg in the sleeping car.* The story was told, and then later told again after the two drinkers had forgotten their telling, but neither time could Frost get the point, so Southern was the accent. *And it was the sort of story I knew I ought to know,* added Frost wistfully. Years afterwards he ran into the Southerner somewhere else and asked him to repeat the story. But though the teller was now sober, Frost could still not get the point.

"Some more bric-a-brac"—the *S* had been written with a long slur. *Sounded drunk,* commented Frost.

It was Harriet Monroe who had given Stevens his start. One got the picture of a rather frail woman boosting a large middle-aged man to an upper level.

NOVEMBER 16, 1954 (Continued)

One of the students asked F. what he thought of Marianne Moore, as if she were in the same class with Stevens.

She's something else again, he said. *An intense Bryn Mawr old maid. She gives nothing for the ear. But she's an intense Bryn Mawr old maid, and that's something.*

He said he thought *Poetry* today was dull. It needed to discover a new star on the horizon. He had told Shapiro so, but Shapiro had asked who was available. The important thing was the discovery and the enthusiasm, not the person discovered.

Other poets were touched on in conversation. (Eliot) His critical lingo had got into his poetry. *Would you use the word* intrigue *in a poem?* ("I might," replied one of the students.) (Pound) His best passage was about the faces in the metro looking like wet petals along a bough. The nicety of that metaphor. Not everyone appreciated it. (MacLeish) He copied St. John Perse's *Anabase* for his *Conquistador.* Didn't deny it, either. Nice fellow, but a dangerous thing to be so carried away with another man's work that you wanted to copy it. (Emerson) "When half gods go the gods arrive." Brilliant but untrue. When half-gods go the quarter-gods arrive. (Whitman) Breadth was his greatness. Whitehead, shortly before his death, had called Whitman America's greatest. (Phyllis McGinley) F. quoted with admiration her line that she was glad there were twelve months, nine muses, and two sexes. Also a recurring line in another poem: "I wish I didn't talk so much at parties."

Other people under discussion were Vrest Orton,[45] Robert Morse Lovett, Reuben Brower,[46] who is now master of one of the Harvard houses.

Frost quoted himself and repeated the quotations. There were two of them, and I'm not sure of the exact wording of either. In answer to the question, Whom do you write for?—*I write for the nice sort of people to whom I belong. Our aim (as poets) is to entertain you with play about what we trust you know already.*

He talked about religion. He had heard that Yvor Winters was asking whether he were a monist or a dualist. His poetry ought to

45. Vrest Orton, Vermont literary man and entrepreneur who, among his many accomplishments, founded the Stephen Daye Press in Brattleboro, Vermont, and the Original Vermont Country Store, a mail-order house in Weston, Vermont.
46. Reuben Brower, see note 14.

answer that. There was almost as much about evil in it as about good. *Good is the better half of evil.* To find out what he believed, one would have to stay around him a long time. He would himself. And the answer would depend not so much on what he said as on how he acted. Unitarians, he maintained, had reverted to the Old Testament and the Jews. Whatever they were, they were not Christians. He told how Allen Tate (a R.C. convert) had introduced him to a certain priest. *And are you a convert?* Frost had asked. *No,* said the priest. *Neither am I,* said Frost with sly malice.

At the beginning of the evening he spoke in disparagement of travel, but then went on to describe what a good time he had had in Brazil and Peru last summer. He was impressed with the honor that South Americans accord to poetry and to all poets. He was sorry he did not have their language, and promised them that he would for his next visit.

OCTOBER 30, 1956

I was awakened by his knock. Although I knew he was coming about 2:00, I had lain down on the couch and dropped off to sleep. Of course I had intended to be outdoors to greet him like royalty when his taxi arrived.

The afternoon was sunny and warm enough for us to sit outdoors for an hour or more. To shelter him from a slight breeze I brought out a large sheet of cardboard that could be set up like a screen. It reminded him of a time long ago when he and Ezra Pound had been saying some of their poems aloud in a London restaurant. Pound had spouted so loudly ("The Goodly Fere") that a waiter had put a screen around them. F. objects to P.'s vile language. F. said to him once, *It comes out of both ends of you, doesn't it?* Then added, *In that way I didn't have to use the word myself.*

A train was going by, and he commented on the whistle. Formerly train whistles disturbed him. Now he likes the sound. I told him that, in answer to complaints, the railroad had changed the diesel snorting horn to something resembling the old steam whistle.

As soon as he arrived, F. spoke of my trees. Had I planted any of the white pines? It was a tree that did not flourish in his Vermont. I called his attention to the wild black cherries becoming prominent near my house. He said he had some black cherry boards stored away for somebody to use sometime. He wondered if he couldn't take part in Senator Flander's program of hardwood reforestation by scooping up rock maple seedlings and setting them out. He hoped in early spring to graft some old apple varieties onto his trees. It is cold enough that far north to make spraying of apples unnecessary. Perhaps the chestnut blight might not reach that far north if he could get some chestnut trees started, though it is beyond the range of the tree.

Mr. F. revealed several interesting biographical facts. Before going to England in 1912 he had almost decided to move to Vancouver. Going to England was with no thought of advancing his literary career. From the sale of his farm he had in all about $3600 and this was enough to take a family of six to England, keep them there three years (in peasant style), and bring them home.[47] Just recently he had learned that it was John Drinkwater who recommended the publication of *A Boy's Will* to David Nutt's widow. D. never revealed this to Frost, though he sent him inscribed copies of his books from time to time. Nor did he ever look up F. when in America.

It was in December 1915 that F. first came to Amherst to give a

47. Lawrance Thompson in his biography of Frost establishes the unreliability of some of the stories Frost told about himself.

reading at Williston Hall, A.C. W. R. Brown[48] was there, deaf even then. In sad state now. Anecdote of B.'s spending most of one day (on an excursion) selecting a boulder for his tombstone and arranging for its transportation to Amherst.

Another early Amherst friend was Lewis[49] of M.A.C., then dean, later president. At a dinner party at President Meiklejohn's, Lewis (a professor of speech) read aloud "The Death of the Hired Man"—the only time anyone ever read one of F.'s poems to his face. This time he didn't mind it, for he had high regard for Lewis.

F. said he had known enough college presidents to be able to put them into two categories: (1) those that had a considered concern for the arts, and (2) those that had a weakness for them. Of the latter, very few. And not including Conant of Harvard.

Three times F. withdrew from his A.C. professorship. In 1920 it was because of the Meiklejohn controversy. He had friends on both sides, and the tension became too great. In 1925 he left because his presence was making Harry DeForest Smith[50] unhappy. In 1938 he parted following an incident with Stanley King.[51] Mrs. F. had just died in Florida and F. himself was gravely ill. King came all the way to see him. Touched, F. said something to the effect that he feared he was more bother than worth. *We won't talk about that—now*, said K. That "now" was what did the harm. As soon as he was well and back north, F. resigned. The underlying trouble, F. now thinks, was a disposition on K.'s part to resent F.'s many friends and commitments outside Amherst. K. was jealous of F., jealous for Amherst.

48. W. R. Brown, Amherst insurance man and realtor, whose telephone number was 1. A staunch friend of Frost.
49. Edward Morgan Lewis, professor of public speaking, and from 1926 to 1927 president of Massachusetts Agricultural College. He next became president of the University of New Hampshire.
50. Harry DeForest Smith, professor of Greek in Amherst College.
51. Stanley King, president of Amherst College, 1932 to 1946.

Mr. F. said he felt he had always fulfilled his academic obligations. But he admitted in himself what he called "a protective laziness."[52]

His sensitiveness to slight came out in another connection. A few evenings ago he went to a certain fraternity to spend the evening. They had tried to get him for several years. The whole bunch greeted him at the door. But one boy said, "You know tomorrow we have exams and some of us may have to leave early. *All right*, F. said he said, *I stay as long as all of you stay*. After about fifteen minutes, one boy slipped out. *Here goes*, cried F., and got up and went. He has his doubts about fraternities. There have been times when an invitation came from a single boy, possibly an unpopular one, and to show their disdain of him, the other boys have treated F. a little cavalierly. Even playing cards as he was speaking. *How are you going to entertain a whole fraternity? I can entertain a nice audience that comes to hear me. But a whole fraternity!*

Recently he had an invitation from Eisenhower to head a committee of intellectuals. Intellectuals! He'd rather be called an intelligentsian. *Do they think I've spent my life writing my one book just to throw it into one of their political campaigns? If I'd known those first little poems I wrote would ever lead to my being asked to head a committee of intellectuals, I wouldn't have written them.* An invitation to head a committee, but never an invitation to dinner. Movie actresses were invited to the White House, but not he. Sherman Adams, a nice man, collects his books. But never an invitation.

Do you know why they don't invite me? They're too honest. They're too decent honest to pretend they are interested in what I am interested in.

As long ago as Coolidge, this invitation to the White House has been a sensitive point. Dwight Morrow tried to get Coolidge to act,

52. Frost's so-called "protective laziness" was mentioned on p. 4 of this book.

but all that C. ever said on the subject was this: *A poet, Dennis McCarthy, used to hang around the State House.*

I had two designs on Mr. F. as we sat there by the pine trees and my little garden, the sun still warm though getting lower and lower. I wanted him to try my flower wine, and I wanted to take his picture. I thought he might be reluctant to do either. But I was pleasantly mistaken. He drank my wine with enthusiasm. And when I proposed some pictures, he stood up with every effort to help.

Strolling about, he remarked that my house was "ship-shape." But he thought he would be lonely living here. I recalled my visit to his Ripton farm in 1943 and how impressed I was with his living arrangements, living on a series of steps, as it were: his solitary cabin at the top of the slope, the Morrison farmhouse lower down where his meals were served and his would-be visitors screened, Breadloaf still farther down where he could go for sociability and tennis, and Middlebury lower still where he could take the train for New York or Boston. He had the freedom to move up or down.

He said he never thought of it that way before.

At one point he got to talking about the "knocking about" he has been doing of recent years. Barre in Vermont, for instance. That marble statue of Burns, carved not by a Scotsman but by an Italian in flight from the Mafia, but killed by the Mafia not long afterwards. A road known as the William Scott Highway in honor of a Union soldier who had gone to sleep on sentry duty but been pardoned by Lincoln. Lincoln more the hero than the poor boy who was saved from execution only to die in battle. And a most forlorn old man who had once had a business of growing and selling wild plants, but who had descended to the point of not even having a shovel.

As soon as we came in, I built a fire in the fireplace. F. had mentioned my being in the *Faber Book of Modern American Verse.* Since he spoke of the book again but hadn't seen a copy, I got out mine and sat beside him on the couch. I had the pleasure of showing him the place of honor of his poem "The Gift Outright." He liked the other selections from his poems too, and made comments on them. Surprised that the Grafton witch rather than the witch of Coös had been chosen. I suggested that Auden might have been influenced by Randall Jarrell's praise of that poem. F. said he had not read what R.J. had written. "Two Look at Two" he had sent to Harper's long ago but it was returned by them. H. S. Canby had advised them that it was not up to F.'s standard. *They haven't got anything of mine since.* "Design," though published rather recently, was written early. "Never Again Would Bird's Song Be the Same" had never been singled out before. He was glad that two of his later poems were included, "The Middleness of the Road" and "Directive." The latter, he said, had been made much of, but the former had aroused little attention.

Then he turned to my poems. He seemed familiar with the first two. When he came to the third, "Apple Peeler,"[53] something remarkable happened. I was still sitting beside him. *Oh,* he exclaimed with a mischievous smile and looking round at me as if he had caught me in the act, *this poem.* At first I hadn't the faintest idea of what he was getting at. But he kept smiling at me and making hints,

53.   APPLE PEELER

> Why the unbroken spiral, Virtuoso,
> Like a trick sonnet in one long, versatile sentence?
>
> Is it a pastime merely, this perfection,
> For an old man, sharp knife, long night, long winter?
>
> Or do your careful fingers move at the stir
> Of unadmitted immemorial magic?
>
> Solitaire. The ticking clock. The apple
> Turning, turning as the round earth turns.

This poem occurs in *New Poems by American Poets* (Ballantine Books, 1953), *The Orb Weaver* (Wesleyan University Press, 1960), and *Come Out Into the Sun: Poems New and Selected* (University of Massachusetts Press, 1965.)

and at last I caught on. He thought I was taking a dig at him in the poem, possibly that the whole poem was really about him. He supposed that his sonnet "The Silken Tent" was the only sonnet in one sentence in the English language. He suspected, therefore, that he was the "virtuoso" turning out "trick" poems after his real inspiration had been exhausted. What a thought! I hardly knew what to say to disabuse him. I didn't deny that I knew about his sonnet and that it might have been in my mind when writing the poem. But I insisted that I had not been thinking of him in particular, certainly not trying to disparage him, or that I used the word "trick" in a disparaging sense even as applied to the actual apple peeler. I could see he was not entirely convinced. *Mr. Frost*, I said, *your poem 'The Silken Tent' is as beautiful as anything you ever did, and there is no trick about it. As for sonnets in one sentence, David Morton does them all the time.*

He does, does he? asked F. with the trace of mischief in his smile. *Then that makes it all right.*

We looked at Gibson's poem "David," the last line of which "Of course, we tell him what we can" F. has always especially admired. *Would make a good motto over an educational institution*, he remarked. *In place of* VERITAS.

Turning a few further pages, F. made gloomy comment on some of his fellow poets:

Winters: *There's my enemy.*
Engle: *There's a man who has disappointed me.*
Roethke: *Insane half the time.*
Agee: *I knew that boy. Committed suicide.*
Dachine Rainer: *A woman's name? Where does she hang out?*

The Bible a great book. *Why was Ananias killed? Not for lying. We all do that. But for holding out on the commune. What is the greatest whodunit in the Bible? The immaculate Conception.* (Apparently he was confusing the Immaculate Conception with the Virgin

Birth.) *A god did it*. He had written a poem on that ("The Bearer of Evil Tidings").

I ventured to say that to my mind polytheism, however fantastic, accounted for the facts of life better than did monotheism. In polytheism there was no problem of evil. Any ill event could have several plausible explanations. An enemy god had done it. Or a friendly god was punishing you for some slight to himself or just to test you. Or the gods were not thinking of you at all; they were just having a spat among themselves and you were in the way.

F. mentioned William James' pluralism. I asked if pluralism might not be just a polite word for polytheism. F. said he thought so.

I showed him the poem by William Hinckley[54] of 500 lines, each ending in "ation" and each "ation" different. Although impressed, he was not quite as amused as I had hoped.

And now a good note to end on. F. said what he had been trying was to write a few poems that the world could not deny.

He had come at 2 : 00 and left about 4 : 45. I called a taxi. When it came, I slipped $1.25 into the driver's hand. But F. saw me do it, demanded the money back for me. *I won't forgive you for this*, I said. *I won't you either*, he retorted, adding, *I was going to say 'Damn your eyes.'*

APRIL 24, 1959

Frost was here yesterday afternoon with Sam Morse.[55] He said his first ancestor in America was banished from town for three years

54. William Hinckley, printer by trade and deacon in the West Medford Baptist Church of which my father, Ebenezer Fisher Francis, was pastor from 1911 to 1921.
55. Samuel French Morse, poet and professor of English at Mount Holyoke College, later at Northeastern University.

because of intimacy with an Indian girl. After the time was up he came back with an English wife and all was proper. *He should have stayed with the Indian girl.*

He asked Morse if he slept right through the night without having to get up once. Said he himself couldn't stand bedclothes. Just two sheets over him. At his room at the Lord Jeff there are now always just the two sheets whoever the chambermaid may be. Another touch of home: the walking stick he cut years ago now stands in a corner of his room whenever he arrives.

My daughter[56] *tells people I am a political innocent. But I'm not.* (Peering from under his eyebrows) *I'm shrewd, shrewd.*

Gardiner Jackson, Amherst graduate and one of "Frost's boys." *He's just naturally more noble than anybody else. I don't mind.* Fired by Reuther the other day. Years ago fired by Henry Wallace. Frost to Wallace, *What do you mean firing one of my boys?* Etc.

Senate chaplain came to him about a prayer he is to make. Should it be for perpetual peace? Said President and he were not sure they should pray for perpetual peace. Frost told him he'd tell him some other things to pray for.

Frost was walking through a diningcar recently. The only diner present (white) called out: *Congratulations on your longevity. To hell with my longevity*, retorted Frost. *Read my books.* And the Negro waiters in chorus: *Yah, read his books.*

In a certain Washington club no one recognized him except the Negro elevator boy. Before he could have his dollar breakfast they had to summon the president.

At a train in the South, a black boy: *May I carry your bag, Mr. Frost? How did you know my name? Oh, I'm a highschool boy.*

There's luck in it, he said, but more than luck. A shrewdness. For instance, his decision not to show his early poems in manuscript to

56. Lesley Frost Ballantine (Mrs. Joseph W. Ballantine) Frost's eldest daughter.

William Dean Howells.[57] He thought he might be interested but would be more impressed with the poems in print.

Editors who kept rejecting his early work made him bitter at the time. Later on when he met them and saw what they looked like and were, he forgave them.

When the two men left (after a visit of perhaps two hours), Frost had a bottle of my dandelion wine, a pair of magnifying spectacles I had recently bought, and without my knowing it and perhaps without his knowing it, my recipe for the wine in his pocket.

It began with my serving small glasses of wine. They both liked it enough to want to know how it was made. Frost said he liked anything sweet. So I got out my recipe on U. of M. stationery. To help him read it, I offered my new little oblong magnifying spectacles. Morse liked the appearance of them and Frost seemed to like their efficacy. He admitted they would be a help to him but protested against taking them from me. But I persuaded him. I guess it was just to make the story complete that he went off with the recipe too.

He said he had been an ailing boy. Glasses were put on him. But soon after, being invited to take part in a football game, he tossed the glasses over the fence. And that was the last of the glasses.

As always, Frost was full of talk of well-known people, friends of his of whom he is very fond, who are either communists, or alcoholics, or psychiatric patients, or inveterate do-gooders. *I don't mind*, he says indulgently. One wonders whether his fondness for such is altogether a fondness in spite of and not partly a fondness because of.

"I like a little corruption myself," he was quoted as saying in a recent interview, "if it's amusing."[58]

(Frost didn't go off with the dandelion wine recipe after all. Long afterward I found it tucked inside a book.)

57. See p. 7 in this book.
58. Quoted by Chester Morrison in "A Visit with Robert L. Frost" in *Look* for March 31, 1959.

CONVERSATIONS

1933/1935

THE conversations with Frost that I have records of occurred in two periods. The talks during the 1950's took place mostly in my home, Fort Juniper, three and a half miles from Amherst center and more or less in the woods. Although it was built in 1940, Frost, for one reason or another, did not discover it until nearly ten years later. Having come first perhaps from curiosity, he continued to come because it proved an ideal place for uninterrupted conversation. Another reason, I think, for his coming was his interest in my little house. Perhaps it reminded him of his own cabin in Ripton,[59] Vermont. Here he could see for himself how I lived, indoors and out.

But my first conversations with Frost occurred twenty years earlier, and took place mostly in the Frost home on Sunset Avenue in Amherst. At that time, in the early 1930's, I was still unpublished in book form, a young poet looking for guidance. So Frost took the role of mentor, and much that he said had to do with my own poems and my problems as a poet.

Because the later conversations seem to me more wide-ranging and versatile and more representative of Frost's general talk, I have put them first in this book. The earlier conversations follow.

There were still other talks with Frost that I somehow failed to record; and doubtless a few visits that have slipped from memory entirely. This is true of both the 1930's and the 1950's, as well as of the years between. The gap was partly due to Frost's disassociation with Amherst College from 1938 to 1946.

59. For the location of his Ripton cabin, see p. 36 in this book.

For instance, Frost came once to the Old House by the Brook[60] where I lived from 1937 to 1940, but there is no mention of his visit in my journal. I think it was in the fall of 1937, for I seem to remember autumn leaves. I brought him out in my little second-hand Model-A Ford roadster. Together we poked about among the cobwebs of the eight tiny unused bedrooms upstairs. It was up there that he advanced the theory that this had been a rooming house for people working in the mill nearby. What else was the meaning of the big bell that could be rung from downstairs?

I well remember also an unrecorded visit with Frost twenty years later. I had happened to see him on the street near Converse Library,[61] and my greeting led to his inviting me to lunch that day at the Lord Jeffery Inn. There were just the two of us at a small table. Since the main diningroom was temporarily out of use, we were in a smaller room where the tables were rather close together. All through the meal I had the problem of trying to answer Frost's rather personal questions loud enough for him to hear but not loud enough for the whole room to listen to. He chided vegetarian me for ordering—was it an omelet?—for my main dish. What I had to drink I have forgotten, but Frost had a daiquiri. He was about to go to England to receive honorary degrees from both Oxford and Cambridge, and I was soon to leave for Rome.[62] He spoke of my little honor as if it were comparable to his great ones.

I am sure that there was a second visit, unrecorded, with Frost and

60. An account of my life at the Old House by the Brook may be found in Chapter II of my autobiography, *The Trouble With Francis*.

61. Converse Library was at that time the library of Amherst College. The present library is the Robert Frost Library, at the laying of whose cornerstone President Kennedy spoke a few weeks before his death.

62. I had been given a "Rome Prize Fellowship" by the American Academy of Arts and Letters and the closely linked National Institute of Arts and Letters, providing for me to live during 1957–58 at the American Academy in Rome, an entirely distinct institution.

Hyde Cox; and a second visit with Frost and Samuel French Morse. But the unrecorded visit I remember most vividly took place on June 14, 1959, which was Baccalaureate Sunday that year at Amherst College. Late in the morning a car drove into my yard and three men got out: Frost, Armour Craig,[63] and Alfred Edwards whom Frost introduced as his publisher. For a while we talked about *Vermont Folk Medicine*, which Holt had recently published. Then the three men discussed Frost's recent eighty-fifth birthday dinner in New York at which Lionel Trilling had made a significant and somewhat controversial speech.

Frost remarked that he was now a member of the Holt firm with the privilege of choosing four books a year, two to make money and two not. (I inferred that if mine were to be one of those books, it would be one of the two not to make money.) He asked how I stood with Macmillan. I replied that Macmillan was no longer interested in me, had rejected my current manuscript. It seemed to me that the moment had come when Frost or Edwards would make a proposal. But before that moment could arrive, I said that I was no longer an unpublished poet, that less than a week ago Wesleyan University Press had accepted my poems for publication.[64]

Oh, why did you do that? exclaimed Frost.

I answered that if I was to be published at all, it seemed to me appropriate and fortunate that it would be by a university press concerned more with the quality of a book than with its chances of making money, a press, moreover, that was away from any big city and here in my New England.

The three men left soon afterwards. Though the friendly tone of our conversation had not been marred, Frost was obviously disappointed. As he went out the door he said, *Too late, too late.* This was the last time he was ever in my home.

63. Armour Craig, see note 2.
64. *The Orb Weaver.*

47

Except for my privately published book, *The Face Against the Glass*, I had not had a book of poems published for fifteen years. So it seemed to me a little odd that Frost begrudged my having accepted an offer of publication, and a good offer, after he had sympathized with me in my long wait. Here was one occasion when I felt Frost was at less than his best, and I did not want to record it. But now, in the context of our thirty years of friendship, I feel that this incident may appropriately take its place.

APRIL 4, 1932

Yesterday my little salute[65] to Robert Frost appeared in the *Springfield Republican and Union*. Thus was the first pop-gun fired in my

·

65.   ROBERT FROST IN AMHERST

Robert Frost is here in town again.
I saw him on the street just yesterday,
The grayest, greatest, man of all our men,
Gray the way a great boulder is gray.

Somehow that brief view of his weathered face
Made our thin air a sturdier atmosphere.
Home is a sounder, more enduring place.
Yet airier too, now Robert Frost is here.

Old hopes gleam in the sun as mica gleams,
Granite ledges crop out of despair—
Or so it seemed, and so it always seems
When Robert Frost and I breathe the same air.

Best of all—you've heard ?—he comes to stay.
This is his home now. He is here for good.
To leave us now would be running away.
(I too would stay forever if I could.)

48

private campaign to establish a significant relation with this most significant man in town. Meanwhile my essay, " Robert Frost, Master of Humor,"[66] is about half done.

JANUARY 24, 1933

Today I started a savings account with a ten-dollar deposit; and I met Robert Frost.[67]

MARCH 14, 1933

An eventful day for me. Not merely that I was at the Frosts for lunch and generous talk before and during and after with Mr. Frost. Rather I was more myself, more at ease than formerly, and Frost himself warmed up more and talked grandly. He told a most amusing anecdote about his relation with a former pupil named Kirk. He gave amusing and shrewd characterizations of some of the

---

While he stays, life that breathless fugitive,
Will stay. While he lives, some things here won't die.
And we, breathing his air, may learn to live
Close to the earth, like him, and near the sky.

66. An essay never published.
67. An account of my meeting Frost may be found in my autobiography, pp. 201–203.

---

women poets of today. He wondered if T. S. Eliot were a "scoundrel" or not.

Best of all were certain critical and theoretical ideas. The most important thing about a poem to him is the willfulness of its central idea, a willfulness so persistent that it should compensate for and triumph over a slip or two of technique. Indeed a faulty poem from the technical point of view may be faulty because of the very vigor of its content. Women's poetry, he believes, evinces women's love of playing with their emotions. Masculine poetry shows emotion only when it has to, and gains in force because of its repression. Poetry should be serious but not too serious; it should play with its seriousness. He praised one of my poems for being not too long. Many modern poets, he says, string out their poetry to undue lengths.

The three poems in my volume[68] that he singled out for honorable mention were "Homeward," "Fable," and "Night Train." He has had the manuscript only a day and asked to keep it longer.

Frost is certainly capable of giving a vivid picture of the seamy side of the poetry world, with its politics, its elbowing, its "gangs." As I listened to him, I felt that nothing was worth while but sincerity and hard work.

He assured me that he read and commended my verse not merely to encourage me, but because it interested him and he felt it was better than the usual. Laughingly he told me he was much nicer before he was forty than he has been since, for then he was willing to judge poetry from the poet's point of view and not merely from his own. But actually he has avoided getting sot and hidebound and tries to put himself in the other poet's shoes when reading his work.

68. This was my unpublished collection of poems at the time. "Homeward" and "Night Train" were later included in my first published volume, *Stand With Me Here* (Macmillan, 1936). "Fable" was never published.

Another long talk with Frost this afternoon, probably my last until next fall or winter, for the Frosts leave town next week.

More than once Frost has said of my manuscript volume: *You'll never do lovelier things than some of these.* He singled out the line from "Gargoyle"—"The baby snow that sleeps upon the sill"—for special praise. *It's a daisy,* he said. In adverse criticism he quoted a line from the same poem that he felt had been determined by the rhyme, and in general he thinks my book is too feminine, although he advanced this criticism with many reservations.

I sat for an hour and a half with Frost talking continuously and almost uninterruptedly. He told of going back to California last year for the first time in forty years. He recalled earthquake experiences à propos of the recent quakes. He told anecdotes about his school-teaching. He talked very easily about himself—how restless he was, how easily he could become annoyed by little things that happened—things that other teachers were reported as saying in their classes.

His conversation often turns to some antithesis between the two sexes. Today it was the difficulty men have who teach in women's colleges and the difficulty they have in transferring to men's colleges. The other day he commented on the precosity of girls in poetry, how much more quickly they pick up the poetic fashions of the day. They are quick-growing grafts, whereas boys develop poetic power slowly but from their own roots. The essence of the masculine in poetry is a reticence about personal emotion; the feminine connotes a willingness to be emotional for the sake of being emotional. *Women cry because they like to, men cry only when they can't help it.* Frost thinks Millay's sonnets are sheer calculation.

He advises me to "let my volume lie" until next fall—advice that

51

is not hard for me to follow, for all the poetry and interest in poetry that I have I want to go into Johnny Appleseed.[69]

APRIL 2, 1933

Speaking of Emerson's poem "Give All to Love," Robert Frost said, *But he didn't give all to love. His transcendentalism demanded that friends, home, everything be sacrificed if necessary. The dilemma is unsolvable. Perhaps that is why we have two hands, so that we can hold such opposites.*
   A rhyme should give you the feeling that it was made in heaven.
   You've got to learn to hover.
   His impersonation of a person "smitten" with beauty was very amusing.

NOVEMBER 21, 1933

Last Friday I spent nearly two hours with Robert Frost at his home. I had met him on the street the night before soon after he had arrived from Vermont, and he kindly invited me to see him the next day. I am going to try to record the gist of his discourse. Discourse, I say, rather than conversation, for Frost loves to flow and anything another person puts in is interruption.[70] If the other person has good

69. I was preparing to write a long poem on the half-historical half-legendary Jonathan Chapman, a poem never finished.
70. This is a somewhat different interpretation of Frost's conversation from the one given at the beginning of this book, p. 3.

sense, he keeps still and listens. Picture the poet lolling in a big chair, his hair getting more and more rumpled, and his words billowing on with the freedom and abundance of the ocean.

He began on the subject of stimulants by saying he distrusts anything but outdoor health. As a boy in San Francisco he saw plenty of the other thing. His father was a politician with headquarters in a fine saloon in and out of which Robert passed freely. It was not until his family moved to Lawrence, Massachusetts, that he encountered the idea that there might be anything wrong in drink. In Lawrence from the age of ten to eighteen he was in a comparatively unalcoholic environment. He began to write poetry while working in a large mill there. The earliest poem in his collected volume dates from that time.

But fatigue can be a drug as well as can hard drink. Mr. Frost has a notion he could go through a volume of poetry and pick out the poems written in the morning and those written at night and under fatigue. This idea brought up the problem of what part of one's mind should be used in writing poetry. Frost doesn't like the word "subconscious." He simply says that the creation of a poem begins in a state. In a good poet this state is highly specialized. Only a particular kind of poem will satisfy it. Some poets write verse from a generalized state like the craving for sweet: anything sweet and sugary satisfies them. The true poet can be satisfied with nothing but an expression of his particular mood which may be very subtle and impossible to analyze. If he allows himself to get switched off, he may achieve a kind of specious success with the poem, but in his heart he will know it is a failure.

Emily Dickinson is a poet whose "state" never gets sidetracked. Since she wrote without thought of publication and was not under the necessity of revamping and polishing, it was easy for her to go right to the point and say precisely what she thought and felt. Her technical irregularities give her poems strength as if she were saying,

---

Look out, Rhyme and Meter, here I come. Frost likes this wilfulness, this unmanageability of the thought by the form, but he thinks it was a little too easily arrived at by Emily Dickinson in whom it is sometimes indistinguishable from carelessness. In other words, she gave up the technical struggle too easily.

Frost remarked about the scarcity of English rhymes, the unavoidability of a poet's repeating his rhymes; but the situation is relieved by the fact that it is not so much words as phrases that rhyme, and phrases are endlessly varied.

The essential idea in verse, i.e., the breaking of lines into uniform lengths, gives a poet something hard to "crack" his sentences over. Our fondness for pentameter he thinks is largely habit and tradition and he scouts Housman's footnote in *The Name and Nature of Poetry* to which I called his attention.

His opinion of Housman is very low. Brainless, he calls him. A dry, classical scholar on the one hand, and a very limited poet on the other. Frost dislikes both the suicidal mood and the pretty technique. *The Name and Nature of Poetry* made him mad, he said. Especially did he dislike what Housman said in disparagement of metaphor (something I had not noted in my reading). Metaphor, Frost is fond of maintaining, is the essence of poetry and if Housman weren't so brainless—this is Frost's attitude—he might see it.

Another scholar with a neat little mind was Mr. Pease (once "President"), Mr. Pease who has *a nice little prose style*. Pease once said to Frost on this subject of metaphor that he could understand how it was desirable now and again to introduce a metaphor into a poem. Frost replied that he had never thought of metaphor in that way, as something to stick in like sticking cloves in a ham.

David Morton was another one to take a whack, I mean to take it in the sense of getting it. Frost had clipped out one of Morton's poems from a newspaper. He read it as a conspicuous example of bad form. I confess I had thought of Morton as being strong in this thing perhaps to the exclusion of much else. But Frost means by form proportion, proportion of thought and its proportioning in the poem. Morton had given too much space to an incidental thought, besides using, as I could see, rather undistinguished language.

I think Morton was introduced into the discourse, however, as an example of limited scope. This thing Frost finds common among young poets. They haven't range enough. They see only one or two kinds of beauty. He told me about a Dutch poet, Van Dorn, whom he used to know and who used to boast of his avoidance of conventionally pretty subjects.

Perhaps it was mention of this old acquaintance that brought another to Frost's mind, Edward Thomas. It was Frost who started Thomas to writing poetry in those years in England, although Thomas had written much prose, and although it was sometimes thought that the Englishman influenced the American as much as the other way round. Evidently Frost had been very fond of his melancholy and unhappy friend, too fond to have done much thinking about him in the fifteen years since Thomas's death in battle. (I recalled Frost's sonnet to him among his collected poems, but I had not known to whom it was addressed.) Thomas was a shy, sensitive, feminine man seemingly fated to be misunderstood and not wholly through the fault of other people. Yet he was strongly built and a brave soldier. I saw his picture, heard extracts from a letter, and was given his collected poems to read.

Finally mention was made of my own poems, my new ones. I was asked to read several. I left the volume[71] with Frost to look over at his leisure. He asked if he might send some of them about to acquaintances. Such kindness! And such a help it will be, this "enlarging of my public," although I was told that it would not be aimed at publishing.

71. The same "volume" as in note 68.

55

Frost says I have the foundations, a musical ear (different from the ear of a musician), an ability to fit sentences and lines together, and style. He seemed surprised that some of my things that I had sent out had not been taken, especially in view of people supposedly looking for new talent. He felt my poems were "carried through" in distinction from much contemporary writing.

I thought as I came away from the house that I had been given help of a kind and an authority that I could have perhaps received from no other man in America.

DECEMBER 18, 1933

Yesterday was a memorable day for me. Over the radio music by Wagner, Beethoven, Rimsky-Korsakoff, Schumann, Mozart, and Brahms (the order in which I heard them). And then in the afternoon a visit with Mr. Frost, the best yet. He said so many good things that I shall find it hard to gather them all together here.

He had had my new volume of poems for a month and began the conversation by asking me how many had been published. When I told him how many I had sent out and how no one of them, the new ones, had been taken, he seemed surprised, and yet not surprised, for his knowledge of the ways of editors and publishers is wide and realistic. Getting poetry accepted he thinks is largely a matter of meeting the right person in the right mood. One must strike while the editor is, if not hot, at least warm. Frost's own usual counsel to wait and then wait some more before trying to have things published, he realizes, may mean waiting until interest has cooled. Consequently whenever a young poet has an opportunity to be published, Frost is careful to stand aside. He told me of his experience with the young

Dartmouth poet, Flaccus, and of an earlier experience with the Middlebury poet. Malam, in whom for a time John Farrar took such an interest. The mention of Farrar called to his mind the astonishing success of Hervy Allen's *Anthony Adverse*. Allen began in poetry and still is chiefly interested in poetry, Frost thinks. It will be interesting to see what effect his success in the novel will have on his poetry. His earlier verse Frost characterized as "scattering."

Anthony Adverse linked the names of Allen and John Theobald.[72] Frost said, *Of course it's a great help if you can work in a copulation or two, at least a deferred copulation. The market value of copulations has gone up, like General Motors.*

As always, this delicious gossip of Frost is more than gossip. It is the pointing of a moral and the adorning of a tale. He said of Harold Vinal,[73] *Whenever I make exception to my usual practice of not offering gratuitous advice, whenever I tell some young poet what I should do if I were he, the answer always is that Harold Vinal told him to do the opposite.* Frost is canny and doesn't make enemies unnecessarily. He says Harriet Monroe is a good friend of his, but always jealous of his discovering new poets. He can write as much as he likes, but let him try to introduce another writer to her, and she is resentful. He could not interest her in Edward Thomas, now an established reputation. Thomas, he admitted, died at just the right time to become famous. I had been reading Frost's copy of Thomas's collected poems, and told him I hoped to have the opportunity sometime of telling Frost how much I liked them. Arthur Guiterman was mentioned as having written tons of verse but as always writing like a school marm. But perhaps the most interesting little portrait was of Frost's "composer-friend" (so called), Charles Walker (I am not sure of the name.) A *rara avis*, a composer with a very special reputation, obsessed with

72. John Theobald, a young English poet then teaching at Amherst College.
73. Harold Vinal, poet and editor of the poetry journal, *Voices*.

the attempt to be utterly original and purified of every influence. He paints, having learned the knack from watching Rockwell Kent. But, says Frost, he swears better than he does anything else. A sort of swearing it is that does not offend you because it is so pure and delicate, and yet with a physical lustiness about it.

From all this anecdotal material the moral might be: if a chance comes to publish, take it; but if the chance doesn't come, don't let it worry you. Waiting often brings better results.

He said I should be content for a while in having even a few people to read and understand and enjoy my poetry. He said again how much Mrs. Frost and he had liked many of them. I told him that I would set those two against the whole world of indifferent editors.

All this, however, was preliminary. The body of the conversation had for its text a statement that went like this: *Of course you've got to be true. I like 'true' better than 'sincere.' But you've also got to cut a caper. You've got to go on a little spree (from the French 'esprit') in each poem. You don't get any fun unless you play with your poem in some way*. He thinks that many young poets lack this feeling for the spree, the caper. They just say straightforwardly what they have to say. My poems, he says, do show a love of cutting a caper. He said something about my knowing a lot about poetry, meaning the craftsmanship of it, and wondered how long I had been writing.

I confess the most valuable part of my visit was when Frost was criticising my own poems. No other person has ever made me feel that he understood all that I had put into the poem, and sometimes it seemed that he saw a little more than I saw. He read slowly with comments, "The Wall," "It Is a Little Thing To Die," "Comet," and "The Hound."[74] Of the second he said, *You know how to draw a fine wire edge over your gizzard. You've got to do that*, he said. (These

74. The four poems mentioned are in my first published volume, *Stand With Me Here*.

mono-rhyme poems which I liked and like so much had brought no enthusiastic response from anyone else.) He did not hesitate to tell me things he did not like. He did not like the opening line, "Thought is a muscled thing" and its repetition in the poem, "Thought," although he thought the rest of it good. *Bad* was what he said of the ending of "Artist"—*people don't talk that way. It's arty.* I told him I had already changed the ending to something quite different.

The subject of inaccuracies in matters of fact came up. I spoke of several of my poems that I had partly come to dislike for this reason. Mr. Frost then told of an experience of his own in the ending of his poem, "The Mountain." Someone had told him that he was mistaken in his description of the handling of the team of oxen. But an old farmer, whom he asked about it afterwards, confirmed what he had written. Frost, though very careful in such things, does not place an exaggerated importance on mere factual accuracy.

Frost would like to see young poets finding their satisfaction in writing rather than in publishing. While they are young, let them enjoy writing for the sake of writing. There will be time enough later on when the passion for publishing has hardened and become domineering. Frost himself feels a dual attitude toward publication. He wants to be published, yet he shrinks from it because it disturbs his tranquility. It takes six months to a year for him to get over a book, that is, to recover from the influence of a book's publication, and to be fresh and unprejudiced for later work. As for me, Frost does not feel that I have a volume yet, only a miscellany.

The indifference of so many editors to my work may be the result of a wrong notion on their part of what poetry is. Disdain of the bourgeois, far from being an earmark of true poetry, has today become a commonplace cliché. Yet editors still look for something precious and disdainful in verse and when they find it, take it believing they have the real thing. Frost says that if his poetry has anything super-rarified about it, he hopes it will remain hidden. He would like to be able to put in a word or two in any group of business men without having them look at each other in embarrassment. So much for "pure poetry."

I am surprised, looking back, that so much was said in a not too long visit—an hour and a half perhaps. On leaving Mr. Frost gave me as a Christmas card a new poem, "The Lone Striker," published as a leaflet.

So ended this very valuable, very entertaining visit.

FEBRUARY 13, 1934

My visit with Frost last Sunday was as entertaining, if not quite so stimulating, as previous visits. It was the third time I had been there since his recovery from his illness. Late in January I dropped in for a few minutes with Porter Dickinson, but I had my first real session with him last Tuesday—a week ago today.

On Sunday he compared himself with Emma Goldman. Both are anarchists, he said, but whereas Emma Goldman believes that society can be based on anarchy, he, Frost, knows better than that and prefers to have his anarchy reserved for himself. Seriously, however, he scorns the idea of being good from inner or outer compulsion. He says he has always done as he pleased through having been drawn to it.

Frost chafes at the contemporary sport of Puritan baiting. He is an admirer of Puritan character and achievement. Reading about the ovation accorded to the debut of "Merry Mount" at the Metropolitan last Saturday almost spoiled his day. He has been reading about the reign of Charles II, and supposes that if we were subject to some of the effects of Charles's anti-Puritan practices, we might find his gay naughtiness less picturesque. He traces the present lingering dislike of New Yorkers and Mainers by people in Vermont to early crookedness in real estate by the courtiers of Charles II.

He mentioned a recent visit from Walter Prichard Eaton at which Eaton had defended a high-fallutin poetic diction. Strange, Frost commented, coming from so Yankee a fellow as Eaton. Carl Sandburg had also been in the other evening and sung him a "low-down" song.

Before leaving I promised to send him the references in the Bible to the statement about "the stone that the builders rejected etc."[75] a passage that appeals particularly to him. He asked to keep my manuscript of "summer" poetry longer in order to show to someone who might drop in.

MARCH 10, 1934

I went to see Mr. Frost yesterday afternoon and was treated to a most interesting stream of reminiscences. Frost revealed himself to me as a man who has stuck to his poetry and to his family, but who has been ready to quit anything else that got in his way. Factory work, farming, newspaper work, teaching—these occupations he walked out on. He went to England chiefly and almost exclusively to get away. His meeting literary people there and his getting a start in publishing were accidental. He told me of those chance meetings that turned out so significantly. But before he went to England, long before,

75. "The stone which the builders refused is become the head stone of the corner." (Psalm 118:22, King James Version.) Matthew (21:42), Mark (12:10), and Luke (20:17) all tell of Jesus' quoting this passage, the word "refused" becoming "rejected."

when he was scarcely more than a boy, he had made another promising beginning with the editors of the *Independent*. Frost himself, however, was too independent to get on with them. He couldn't make himself like their idol, Lanier. Those years of neglect that followed, however, performed an important function: they left him free to slough off everything that was not central to himself. When he finally achieved recognition, his poetry was a unified body.

MARCH 13, 1934

This noon I had lunch with Mr. Frost.

This afternoon Frost talked about Hulme, the English philosopher, Edward Thomas, W. H. Davies, Ralph Hogdson, T. S. Eliot, Irving Babbitt, Carl Sandburg and others including less celebrated and nearer contemporaries. Frost had a long talk with Babbitt shortly before the latter's death this summer. Babbitt told Frost that T. S. Eliot addressed him as "master" in his letters while saying unpleasant things about him at other times. "Dirty" was the expression used by the American humanist of the English humanist.[76]

At the mention of Gertrude Stein (an amusing review of her opera that I had just read), Frost said the moderns were simply taking seriously what we had always used to take as funny. I said that the modernists retaliated by taking as funny what we had always regarded as serious.

He touched on his religious views. He has always believed in God and has never been troubled with religious doubts. He admits his thinking is "wishful" thinking, but in a good and necessary sense as equivalent to an expression of will. The wish is not a creative wish but a realizing wish, he believes.

76. "English humanist" is scarcely the term for Eliot.

America is not going to be ruined by anything that the present administration does or doesn't do. I asked whether that hard-minded view might not be well extended to the world which has survived some pretty violent stresses and strains during the past millions of years.

By the way, we had a delicious lunch—chops, mashed potato, peas, bread and butter, cranberry sauce, pickles, ginger ale, lemon meringue pie, and two kinds of ice cream ! Mr. Frost and I were alone at the table. Mrs. Frost is in Montana where her daughter is expecting a baby. The lunch was proof that Mr. Frost is being well taken care of in his wife's absence.

MAY 27, 1934

Yesterday I also called briefly on another man and his wife who had true occasion for grief.[77] It was the first time I had seen Mr. and Mrs. Frost since the recent death of their youngest daughter, a death surrounded by circumstances peculiarly distressing to the parents. They had reason to look worn and grief-stricken.

JUNE 11, 1934

A week ago Friday I had a session with Frost. Although I was suffering from a severe cold (fool I was to go in such a condition), a cold that

77. This entry is an unfortunately abrupt and inadequate mention of the agonizing tragedy surrounding the death of Marjorie Frost Fraser, Frost's youngest daughter.

laid me up for a week and from which I have not yet entirely re-
covered—I think I have never been more moved by Mr. Frost's conversation than I was that morning. Certainly he has never been more
luminous and kindly.

I had told him of the series of disappointments I had just had regarding editors and publishers, and much that he said was by way of
consolation, although he explicitly denied that he was doing that. *Of
course*, he said, *you can always get better. There is always room for
improvement in any poet;*[78] *and if publication is deferred, you have a
chance to be more selective.* He said he was really glad that he had had
to wait for publication, and he admitted that he was not ashamed of
the way he had taken the waiting. He went on living and writing and
did not regard his failure with the publishers too seriously. But there
did come a time when he gathered his forces together in an effort to
force the publishers to recognize; he places that turning-point in his
morale at the time when he gave up farming for a return to teaching.

*You'd like to have every part of your poem related to every other
part, wouldn't you?* he said.

And that's what you mean by form, isn't it, Mr. Frost? I asked.
Yes, he said.

JUNE 13, 1934

Yesterday afternoon I went round to the Frosts' for my last visit of
the season. When I left I told Mr. Frost he had given me enough to
live on for the next five or six months. And that was the truth.

He began by asking about my living quarters, and that subject

78. Frost seemingly later changed his mind about this, as told on p. 19 of this book,
and also on p. 85.

naturally led to some talk about Mrs. Hopkins[79] and her antique shop. He thought it unusual that a woman from the South should have her flair for business. Upon a reference from me to the opening lines of his "New Hampshire," he told me that the woman from the South there referred to was the wife of a well-known Harvard professor, and that the woman had never recognized herself in his poem.

Some turn of the conversation gave me an opportunity to ask him frankly the question that had been in my mind for a week: Should I return to teaching? I gave an account of the teaching I had done, my reasons for leaving that work, and my reasons for wanting to return to it.

In answer he did not commit himself right away. He described the experiences of a young teacher he had known in his own teaching days—a fellow who had failed to achieve any sort of discipline over his classes, but who had after a number of years out of teaching during which he worked at very humble jobs, managed to jump from public school teaching to teaching in the graduate school of the University of Wisconsin. Frost met him there quite unexpectedly and ironically during a poetry reading. Nothing was said about the dark past, Frost chuckled.

As an example of the other extreme of teacher, the vigorous indomitable type that treats the pupil roughly rather than gets treated roughly himself, Frost mentioned Cornelius Weygandt, the author of a number of books in prose, the latest of which, *The White Hills*, I happened to have out from the library. A big, enterprising, energetic man he is, who finds time aside from his teaching to write extensively of his native Pennsylvania as well of New Hampshire where he has summered for many years, and who is a chicken fancier to boot. He too occurs in "New Hampshire."

79. Mrs. Hopkins, wife of Arthur John Hopkins, professor of chemistry in Amherst College. As Margaret Sutton Briscoe she had been a successful short story writer. I lived in the Hopkins home as helper from June, 1933, to August, 1935.

Frost's own teaching has been varied and interesting. While a student at Dartmouth he suddenly made up his mind to go home and relieve his mother from teaching a class of overgrown, troublesome boys. College life was one rough-house after another. Why not put rough-housing to a use? He entered that school room ready for trouble and even looking for it. He had a bunch of ratans that he had bought with his own money, and they were used. He laid out one fellow after another, and got some order back into the room. (Only the girls gave him trouble, one in particular. Unfortunately he could not break *their* necks.) But the strain of ruling was great. He had to lie down and rest a couple of hours each day after he got home. And though he succeeded in straightening out the unruly bunch of boys, it did not make him popular in town where the men preferred to hear stories of pupil prowess.

Except for two years at Pinkerton Academy (incidentally the two most unproductive years of his life), his teaching had been mostly in a little one-room country school—a job he could get any time he wanted it, and that was almost like home.

As for me, he thought a job would do my writing good, but he advised a job as far away from writing as possible. He said he was confident I could write, but that my "book" could still stand some more squeezing. And then he came to Louis Untermeyer's visit.

He was disappointed, he said, with Mr. Untermeyer's attitude toward my work. He thought the poem nice, but showed no enthusiasm, as Frost had hoped he would. Untermeyer, Frost thinks, for all his own enthusiasm about poetry, has become a little hardened to the poetry of other people. He answers only one letter in ten (letters, that is, from struggling poets), and isn't too sensitive to their struggles. Roberta Swartz,[80] the Mount Holyoke poet, met Untermeyer (at Frost's) at just the right time for him to get her first book pub-

80. Roberta Swartz, see note 36.

---

lished by Harcourt. But when she had her second book ready, he was not interested. Nor was Harcourt. Fortunately Miss Swartz entertained a woman from Harper's about that time, and the acquaintance resulted in Harper's taking her second book. Frost's comment was to the effect that it was a pretty hard life when poetry had to be published in that hook-or-crook way.

As an illustration of the hardness and fallibility of both critics and publishers (Untermeyer and Harcourt in particular), Frost recalled Edward Thomas. Untermeyer now includes Thomas in his English Anthology, and ranks him almost as high as any recent English poet. But years ago when Frost was trying to gain some acceptance for Thomas in America, Untermeyer was not interested (although he has conveniently forgotten that he was not interested), and Harcourt did not hide the fact that he was publishing the poems as a personal favor to Frost. *We can afford to do one book for your sake, Robert.* Frost does not forget his hurt feelings.

Right now Untermeyer's three enthusiasms are Spender, McCord, and MacLeish. Frost knows and likes McCord and his poetry, but thinks a fondness for doing stunts with rhymes impairs the poems. A curious thing it is that McCord living in Cambridge and knowing everybody of importance, has never yet got a poem into *The Atlantic*. MacLeish is, to Frost, one of the tough boys of the Hemingway school. He pictured MacLeish's disgust at the Edna Millay sort of feminine poetic posturing, but thought MacLeish rather went to the other extreme. Frost seems to have disposed of *Conquistador* to his own satisfaction by tracing it to two books he saw in MacLeish's library, one that gave the substance of the poem, the other (a French work) that gave the technique. MacLeish's mode of writing poetry out of his reading led Frost to speak of some early poems of his own, also based on reading and quite out of his true manner. The first poem he ever wrote was a long affair about the conquest of Mexico, published in the high school paper. Frost knows that must have been bad. Others were better but are better hidden—one about Columbus still trying to get through to India and finally slipping through the Panama Canal without ever suspecting it was anything but *the* long-sought passage; another about the ships of Caesar blown westward from Britain into the sunset.

This writing out of one's reading and memory also brought up the name of a certain young little-known poet whom Frost regards as one completely at sea. His long poem Frost compared to what the Cyclops vomited up—scraps from many sources, ill-digested and still distinguishable.

I fear my own proferrings are equally miscellaneous, but Frost gives me grounds for some assurance and as much hope as perhaps I need. Picking up my *Men in the Landscape*,[81] he divided his time between the good and the bad. What is bad is chiefly a certain unreality, a posing, a literary quality. Such is the "arrogant boots" in the poem "Roots," and the entire first stanza. He called my attention to my fondness for beginning sentences with "let" and the feeling of the rhetorical and churchly that it gave, as in "Let us pray." He referred to the sonnet "Kneel by your chair like an obedient child," and I was ashamed to recognize at this late date what a bad thing it is. I think I got a wholesome shock that will make me more closely critical of my work and may provide a spur for new work that will prove tenable.

The poem "The Hound" he likes with reservations. "Living Things," "Slow Things," and especially "Homeward" he commended.[82] He called "Homeward" flawless and said that anybody who didn't approve of that poem didn't know what poetry was.

Before I left he spoke again of my teaching and advised me not to return to it, not for a while anyway. He said something about being

81. See note 68.
82. The four poems mentioned were later included in *Stand With Me Here*.

grimly sure that I could make a go of it as a writer. He told me that
Mrs. Frost felt that way and that she knew as much about such things
as Louis Untermeyer did. The main thing is to be dead in earnest
that you mean everything you say, even though poetry is playing
with meanings. He said he sometimes put it this way: making believe
something is so that is so. (I fear I haven't quite got his words.)

No visit with Mr. Frost has done me more good than yesterday's
did. I am ready to go on, and I think I can go on.

JUNE 14, 1934

Mr. Frost said he admired my poem "Cloud in Woodcut"[83] except
for one word, the word "high" in the line "Teach your knife high
compromise." He said the word sounded "throaty." What a shrewd,
incisive criticism !

Later in our conversation he defined my greatest danger as
preciousness.

NOVEMBER 8, 1934

A visit with Frost, my first since his return from Vermont a month
or so ago. He began by speaking of Mr. A.,[84] the Unitarian minister,
who had just been there—a man with a mind but a restless, agitating
sort of man. A little confused, not clear in his symbols. Thought life

83. "Cloud in Woodcut" is also in *Stand With Me Here.*
84. The Reverend Barton Akley was pastor of the Unitarian Church in Amherst
from 1930 to 1937.

was a calamity, or at least calamitous. Perhaps a frustrated poet without knowing it. A poet who had not risen above the argumentative level which is just below the level of the perception of wholes—which is art. I told Frost that A.'s characteristic equipment as he walked down the street was a pipe in his mouth and a red beret on his head.

Frost admitted that life might be looked upon as calamitous, but that his own attitude was a constant measuring up rather than a measuring down from a distant and impossible ideal. Starting with nothing, he was always impressed with what life offered. Life was for him not a "rising on the stepping stones of one's dead self" but a slow accumulation. Of Emerson, whom Frost probably regards as America's greatest poet, he said that one needed to watch out for flaws in his thinking. "The half-Gods" do not go. I said that to me Emerson was concerned only with the light, the day; that if we made allowances for this disregard of the negative, the evil, the night, we need not be misled or disappointed in Emerson.

I had taken with me a typewritten copy of all of Frost's poems printed in magazines since his last volume, and I asked him if my list was complete. He told me of a poem I had not known of, "Clear and Colder," which he had "given" to some "boys" who had a magazine called *Direction* out in Illinois. He hid his generosity by saying that a few poems printed in obscure magazines would give his next volume that many poems that would be new to the general reader. Then whimsically he added, *Sometimes I think I won't have another volume but will let my children publish a volume after I am dead at the age of ninety*. He was getting tired of publishers and publishing and all that they involved; but not of poetry. He recalled a similar mood when he went to England: he had so lost touch with the world of current published poetry that he had never even heard of Ezra Pound or Walter de la Mare.

He asked me which of his new poems I thought best. I laughed and hesitated, then mentioned two, "Not Out Far Nor In Deep" and "Two Tramps in Mud-Time." I told him the first had grown on me. Of the second he said it was probably the best of the lot, had more to it. I said something about its exuberance and effortlessness. Frost contrasted his idea in the last stanza:

> My object in living is to unite
> My avocation with my vocation
> As my two eyes make one in sight—

with the popular American ideal of having one hour of drudgery with twenty-three hours of play. Frost wants his play and drudgery inextricably mixed. *That's what we do in a poem*, I said, *why not in living?*

Other recent poems were spoken of. He thought "The Lone Striker" for a talking poem was one of the best. Someone had suggested his changing the title of "They Were Welcome to Their Belief" to one of the other lines. He had felt a little doubtful about "Moon Compasses," its final, sensitive, almost hesitant line. Was something more expected? Nothing more ever came. Also doubtful was the bitter tone of "Provide, Provide" whose best stanza he picked as this one:

> No memory of having starred
> Makes up for later disregard
> Or keeps the end from being hard.

Mr. Frost said he was seldom news. When he goes to a city, New York or any other, he has a good audience, but not much is said about it in the papers the next day. The reporters come to him for a resumé of his speech, but this he can never give for he never knows just what he is going to say, certainly not how he is going to say it. He invites the reporters to come and listen for themselves, but they say they can't; they have a bean supper to go to. So the speaking or the reading is not reported, unless perhaps Louis Untermeyer says something saucy or timely. It may be just as well as it is, although he would like

---

71

to make more stir. There is not much hostile criticism; but what there is he must protect himself from. A careless jibe at "West-Running Brook" that he chanced upon in a newspaper left its poison in him. Once he had occasion to say that Swinburne had fewer "speaking tones" than any other English poet, and that the wave-like surge of his rhythm tended toward monotony. Well, some ardent lover of Swinburne took offense and let it be known the next day in her review of the speech.

Mr. Frost returned to me the volume of verse he has had during the summer (this was my "omnibus" once squeezed), and I left him with the volume that I sent Professor Post (which had been squeezed the second time). I had also added six new poems. I showed him Post's[85] letter of criticism which he read with mingled amusement and disgust and swore at the end. Had I paid this fellow so much a line for his criticism? He recalled having once hired some criticism long ago on a poem that happened to have one sentence extending through two stanzas. The critic merely remarked that such was an unusual thing to do!

In leaving I said that I was getting so adept in "squeezing" that I didn't know I had anything left. He came out on the porch and replied that there wasn't a poem in that whole bunch (referring to several recent volumes by young American poets that he had showed me) that was equal to the least of mine. Well, I couldn't swallow that, said I was going to forget it. But I haven't forgotten it.

Frost had come across my poem "Roots" reprinted in the *New York Herald Tribune* some time ago—I don't know when. I showed it to him in the *V.Q.R.*,[86] and told him that its revised form was due wholly to his criticism last June.

85. Post was a professor of English in the Boston area, with whom I had been put in touch through a friend of mine, and who graciously consented to "evaluate" some of my poems.
86. "Roots" appeared in the *Virginia Quarterly Review*, October 1934.

He left with me the comforting thought that no abandoned poem is ever really lost; it will enrich one's future work. He said there were lines in "Two Tramps in Mud-Time" that went back twenty years.

A bit of irony while I was still taking leave of him on the porch: join the Archibald MacLeish–T. S. Eliot gang and you will get published.

Mr. Frost invited me to come again before too long for he plans to spend the winter in the South, and thereby break his two-year habit of getting ill. I was surprised to hear him say that he had as many interruptions in South Shaftsbury as he does in Amherst; at least one thing a day, and that is enough to break up a day for him. He escapes people only when he is in Franconia escaping hay fever. His two lectures at Amherst College on "What Poetry Thinks" are scheduled for April.

He was interested in hearing about John Andrews'[87] job at Beloit. He had been near there recently. This fact and the interruption of my visit by the arrival of Miss Snell[88] of Mount Holyoke led him to speak of an experience Gordon Chalmers,[89] the new young president of some Middle-Western college, is having in meeting political corruption.

I was there less than an hour and a half, and half an hour of that time Frost was with his other callers and I was alone, yet how much there is to remember.

87. John Andrews, son of Charles Andrews, treasurer of Amherst College. He at the piano and I with my violin once gave Frost a brief concert in the Frost home. A student of philosophy at the time, Andrews later and for many years was professor of philosophy in Middlebury College.
88. Ada Laura Fonda Snell, professor of English in Mount Holyoke College.
89. Gordon Keith Chalmers, see note 36.

Last Monday I had my first session with Frost since last fall. Mrs. Frost led the conversation to the subject of poultry, and I switched it to poetry by way of the lark and the nightingale. Mr. Frost confessed that he was no bird authority, but admitted that he hadn't written about any bird that he didn't know. He wondered how many he had got in. I mentioned the anonymity of some of his birds, the "Minor Bird" for example. He said it was the orchard robin or the oriole.

Frost's care as to his facts and his love of facts have led some people to suppose that it is the facts that make the poem. He has to guard against this misinterpretation. He spoke of a "one-horse celebrity" living not far from Albany, who writes naturalist poetry. The factual content is so rich and true that the poetry is almost good.

Not fact but form is the key to poetry. As a fine example of form Mr. Frost read aloud Robinson's "Miniver Cheevy." He especially admires the lines

> He thought and thought and thought
> And thought about it.

I had not known that Robinson was a heavy drinker and an omnivorous devourer of newspapers. Frost entertained us (Professor Manthy-Zorn was also present) with Thornton Wilder's impersonation of Robinson.

JUNE 29, 1935

Last Monday afternoon Robert Frost spent two hours in a chair on our side porch. For the first hour he talked to me, mostly about his experiences at Pinkerton Academy. Then Father and Mother arrived, and he talked to us all, mostly about Russia, and mostly to Russia's disparagement.

Robert Frost has pulled my orbit a little nearer to his. He may have pulled me a bit out of my true shape. But the stuff in me is still my own stuff.

———

EPILOGUE

FROST AT EIGHTY

ROBERT FROST in any group makes the other men seem like boys. Whatever their age, he always looks the oldest. No one not profoundly old could in repose look so profoundly sad.

Most men have to prepare what they have to say. Having prepared, some of them speak well. Frost no more bothers to prepare than he bothers to brush his hair. His whole life has been his preparation. Since he can't be caught off guard, he doesn't bother to guard. He has trusted himself so far so long that he now differs from us in kind as well as in degree. He has a dimension of his own. When he speaks, we do not criticize what he says and how he says it. He is. If he stumbles, his stumbling is more eloquent than our dancing.

During the dinner, in spite of the eighty magnificent red roses in front of him, Frost did not smile, did not chat.[90] He was the only person in the room not chatting, not smiling. Mask-like, gray-to-white, infinitely weary, utterly impassive, he seemed a slightly larger-than-life image of himself. A boulder at the beach takes the wash of surf and spray not more indifferently than he took the chit-chat and speech-making. MacLeish, Cole, Untermeyer, and Wilder spoke, but he had heard it all before. Many times before and long ago. They spoke, and he suffered them to speak.

Cole told the legendary story of Frost's giving an *A* to a student who merely signed his name to the examination book. Without looking up, Frost muttered, *It was the only* A *I gave.*

Untermeyer told a legendary story too. He went on, without diffidence, to claim that he had written "The first or second" review

90. I learned later that Frost had not been well and was dining on a soft-boiled egg.

written in America of *A Boy's Will*. In addressing Frost, MacLeish called him, softly, "Robert." Later, when Frost was reading from his poems and seeming to invite suggestions, Untermeyer called him "Rob."

But to Frost it seemed to make less than any difference what they called him or said about him. Even when Thornton Wilder's passionate antics reached a climax in his knocking off with his gesticulating right hand his spectacles and catching them with his left—all without interrupting his oratory—Frost did not blink.

Only with Edward Hyde Cox's speech of presentation (of a Wyeth painting) did Mr. Frost come to life. Cox, a wealthy yet sensitive man, has been for many years a sort of spiritual son of Frost. Though now perhaps forty, he is still as slender as a youth. Facing Frost and speaking very simply and with a delicate earnestness, he told how at a birthday party there should be a present, and how his grandmother had taught him years ago to pick a present that the giver himself would fall in love with, and how the opportunity to have a part in such a gift had overcome his shyness in speaking on such an occasion, and how he hoped—his pleasure being so great, so much greater than his shyness—that he could go on giving Robert Frost birthday gifts for many years to come. A most artfully artless little speech, and beautifully given. Cox had the luck to be and the wit to recognize that he was the perfect foil to the old wizard beside him. The other speakers had been under the disadvantage of trying to say wise things about a wise man. Cox did not try to be wise; he was content to be young and simple and affectionate.

The visible effect on Frost was moving. The gray mask perceptibly mellowed. The great head moved as by a kind of tropism till its gaze met the speaker, and the ghost of a smile, the gentlest imaginable smile, came over the face.

THE ROBERT FROST MEMORIAL SERVICE

Johnson Chapel, Amherst College, February 17, 1963, 2:00 P.M.

President Calvin Plimpton gowned in scarlet and moving with slow strides, the upper half of his long body bent forward as if bearing the full weight of the occasion—followed by the Rt. Rev. Henry Wise Hobson of the Diocese of Southern Ohio in ecclesiastical vestments and looking like the Platonic archetype of Bishop—and Mark Van Doren whose spare figure and academic robe betokened, if not a bishop, at the very least an abbot—mounted the platform.

The ushers had just escorted to their seats in the central front section the last of the special guests of honor. (I say "special guests of honor" since the entire congregation of 700 consisted exclusively of specially invited guests.) Chief Justice and Mrs. Warren, Justice Goldberg, Secretary and Mrs. Udall. Members of the family and intimates. Katherine Morrison, a more than daughter. Leslie Frost Ballantine, one of the two living children of the original six.

Bishop Hobson rose. So simple, so serene, a child might have mistaken him for God Almighty himself. He prayed to God. He entrusted Robert to God's care and specified what God was to do with him. Extraordinary. Extraordinarily beautiful. Just the three of them: Robert, the Bishop, and God.

Later the Bishop read from the Bible, principally from Job which had been of all books of the Bible the book Robert had pondered most profoundly. Perhaps the book of all books. Frost was the Job of our time, to whom much had been given, from whom much had been taken away. Out of great tribulation he had emerged a great believer.

President Plimpton rose. His drooping, almost whining voice became a strangely expressive instrument for the unpompous things he had to say. Like the man he praised he took risks. He said he thought Frost would be amused by this memorial service. But if this was a risk, it was a risk relating to the audience, not to the truth. He could have said nothing more certain. For he did not say—and I trust he did not mean—that Frost would have been *merely* amused. Frost would have been amused because he was amused with life itself. Humor, if we must call it that, was a never-absent ingredient or element that ranged from the broad and wise-cracking to something so delicate it was indistinguishable not only from poetry but from the essence of poetry.

Mark Van Doren read eleven Frost poems. He read well, but what was inspired was not so much his reading as his selection.

Again, for a moment, we had Robert, the Bishop, and God. Then the special guests of honor took their leave while the lesser guests of honor stood and watched them go.

But who was this man who had been sitting in the very center of felicity? A presentiment, a vision of the long line of English poets reaching back through the ages. Surely no one could have been here more fittingly than Hardy?

A moment only—then Francis Biddle took his hat and coat and departed.

FROST TODAY

A READER might prefer this small book to end here—with the death of Frost—arguing that its purpose and justification was to make available all the records of conversations with Frost that Francis had made at the time of those conversations, and that this had now been done.

But if one reader felt this way, another reader might feel differently. He might say that having listened to Frost speaking to Francis in the 1930's and the 1950's, he would like to know what Frost was saying to Francis in the 1970's, and, possibly, what Francis was now saying to Frost. What of Frost today, the man and the poet? I myself am persuaded that this challenge should be met.

From the time I moved to Amherst in September of 1926 to teach English in the high school, I used to see Frost now and then about town. Though I did not meet him till January of 1933, his presence always excited me. Once I caught a glimpse of him through a window as he was walking along a side street with his brisk rolling gait. Another time I went into the post-office and found him there talking with Charles R. Green. I got out as fast and inconspicuously as possible.

Why was I afraid? I was afraid to confront him with nothing to show, nothing to defend myself with. If I had had anything I felt was worth showing, if indeed I had not at the time resented even being called a poet, I should probably have been a bit bolder. On the other hand, if I had not been writing poetry at all, I might have been no more nervous in his presence than I would have been with any other celebrity. It was the uncertainty of my status that made me timid. I did not know how comfortable a person Frost was to meet and how readily he could put another at ease.

By spring of 1932 my attitude had changed, as my entry for April 4 of that year testifies. My verses in the *Springfield Republican*[91] had been written to celebrate his buying a home in Amherst and so being here "for good." How the kindly if redoubtable Mrs. Hopkins the following year used those verses to introduce me to Frost, I have told in my autobiography.[92]

In those years I was rather innocent of the world of contemporary poetry, in spite of my two Harvard degrees. I had scarcely an inkling that the so-called "Poetry Renascence" of Sandburg, Masters, Lindsay, and Frost—whose vivid plainness had brought new readers to poetry—was even then being overtaken by a still newer wave of "difficult" poetry that would overshadow Frost for a long time and would shrink the poetry audience to an elite. I was not aware that Frost who had seemed so new so short a time before would soon be regarded as outmoded by the leading critics.

It may have been just as well. I could take to heart and make use of all that Frost had to offer me without any misgiving. And my own poems could continue to sprout like weeds or wildflowers with no hint of hothouse air.

Having met Frost I ceased to be timid though I remained somewhat in awe of him. Today that awe has long since vanished, leaving admiration for his art and gratitude for his friendship and help. If I could talk with him now, I would ask him questions I never asked, partly because I am somewhat bolder and partly because those questions are sharper in my mind. I should especially like to question some of his notions about poetry, his oft-repeated quip, for example, that writing free verse is like playing tennis with the net down.

Yes, if I could chat with him today, here in my home or in perhaps some less tangible place, I should like to say, "Mr. Frost"—or maybe

91. See note 65.
92. See note 67.

84

I would finally call him "Robert" to his face as I think he sometimes hinted I should—"Robert, there are other games than tennis that can be played on a tennis court, games in which a net would be irrelevant and even a hindrance, yet games fully as exacting as tennis. Further, on a tennis court dancers could dance and for them a net would be only in the way. A modern dancer, you know, is not regulated by rules or other external demands but is guided only by the inner compulsion of his art. I am all with you that art demands a limit, a challenge, but meter and rhyme are not the only available limitations and challenges. Anglo-Saxon poetry did it with alliteration and a strong beat, regardless of the precise number of syllables. Japanese haiku does it by counting syllables themselves, not by grouping syllables into metrical feet. There are many potential ways (including my own technique of 'word-count,') of providing the needed element of resistance. And furthermore, can't the very stuff of a poem be so shaped and molded and formed that a more external and explicit formality would be superfluous? Perhaps it comes down to what one means by 'free verse.' Admittedly verse that is merely free is flabby; but verse that is controlled, though not by meter and rhyme, perhaps should not be called free verse."

I think he would listen sympathetically. He might even give in to me, as he once did on another of his pet notions. As I tell in the entry for October 22, 1952, he had asked me what I had been doing and I said I had been trying to make my poems better. Disdainfully he asserted that poets don't improve, they only change. A poem must be written in one impulse, at one sitting, like a piece of ice on a hot stove that rides on its own melting.[93] But a moment later he admitted that it had taken Gray eighteen years to complete his *Elegy*. I think Frost, if put in a corner, would concede that spontaneity sometimes has to be labored for.

93. See *The Complete Poems of Robert Frost* (1949), the last paragraph of the preface called, "The Figure a Poem Makes."

I should also like to challenge his well-known witticism about the potato. There are two kinds of realist, he said, one that wants the potato with all its dirt clinging to it, and one that prefers the potato scrubbed clean. He himself is for the clean potato. That is what art does for life: "clean it and strip it to form."[94] But Robert, doesn't it all depend on what you are going to do with your potato? If you're going to plant it, you'd never think of scrubbing it first. Instead of doing the potato any good, scrubbing could only do it harm by breaking the sprouts. But if you're going to boil that potato, you or anyone else would scrub it as a matter of course. If you're going to bake it and eat the skin with the rest of the potato, you'd probably do more than merely scrub it. This is not a world in which we choose between dirty and clean potatoes; this is a world in which we need and welcome both. And it's precisely the realist who understands and accepts this fact. Didn't you yourself once say: "It's knowing what to do with things that counts?"

I think Frost would respect my point of view and respect me for speaking it. Writing about me to Louis Untermeyer on February 13, 1936, he said: "Neither I nor anybody else own him or very much influences his thinking. His opinions are no pushovers. He never starts a subject one way and then at the first sign or look of dissent from you steers it another way."[95]

As for Frost's religious views, I might be a bit cautious. If I were too inquisitive about his God, might he not feel I was taking unfair advantage since he could not question me about mine, I who had none? What I could do would be to sketch the God I found in his poems and then ask if this were a true interpretation.

The God in Frost's poems is always outside humanity and some-

---

94. Quoted by Dr. Calvin H. Plimpton in his "Reflections" at the Frost Memorial Service in Johnson Chapel, Amherst College, February 17, 1963.
95. *The Letters of Robert Frost to Louis Untermeyer* (Holt, Rinehart, and Winston, 1963), p. 270. Frost's letter is dated Feb. 13, 1936.

times very far outside, never as with Wordsworth "in the mind of man" as well.[96] He is out beyond the reach of man's telescopes and speculation,[97] and his functions today seem largely residual. Since he does not meddle too much in human affairs, it is fitting for man not to meddle too much with him. "One thing: he didn't drag God into it," exclaims a speaker in the poem "Snow." Though Frost admits that "something has to be left to God,"[98] note that it is only *something*.

When the fugitive Jonah (*A Masque of Mercy*) "hatless in a whirl of snow," bursts into the bookstore and into the poem with the cry: "God's after me!" the effect is startlingly comic, since such behavior would be most unbecoming of God. "God's after me!" cries Jonah; and Jesse Bel aptly retorts: "You mean the Devil is." But note: though God comes unusually close to man at this point, he is still outside.

When Lawrance Thompson was in Amherst in June of 1971, he asked me among other things if I had ever argued with Frost over religion. The question is significant. That Thompson argued with Frost whereas I never did points up the difference between us both in personality and in position. As a biographer, *the* biographer, it was imperative for Thompson to dig relentlessly into his subject, all the more so since his passion for biographical truth was not always shared by Frost. I picture Frost as Proteus, the Old Man of the Sea, emerging

96.   And I have felt
        A presence that disturbs me with the joy
        Of elevated thoughts: a sense sublime
        Of something far more deeply interfused,
        Whose dwelling is the light of setting suns,
        And the round ocean and the living air,
        And the blue sky, and in the mind of man:

Wordsworth, "Lines composed a few miles above Tintern Abbey, on revisiting the banks of the Wye."
97. See Frost's poem, "I Will Sing You One-O."
98. Line from "Good-by and Keep Cold."

at noon to seek the coolness of some rocky cave. Though he knows the truth, he will not utter it unless caught and pinned down. But first, to confuse his captor, he goes through a series of disconcerting changes, transforming himself into fire, wind, wild beast, etc. If his captor holds on, Proteus will finally acknowledge defeat and speak the truth.

The nearest I ever came to arguing with Frost about religion was over his poem " Directive."

Under a spell so the wrong ones can't find it,

So can't get saved, as Saint Mark says they mustn't.[99]

But I have already given an account of that episode.

How could so distant and indifferent a God be at the same time so stern a judge of man's shortcomings, as Frost maintains he is ?[100] And how reconcile the comic Jonah with his cry, " God's after me ! " with the sublime Hound of Heaven whom Frost as a young man had found so impressive ?

If Frost in turn asked me about my own views, I could now cite my autobiography in the last chapter of which I had at last got some of those views stated. I could point out that in that chapter the question of God is largely bypassed. Most religious arguments start with God; if the existence of God is established, then the problem of evil is half-solved; for though we human beings may never find the solution, we can trust that in the mind of God such a solution exists. By contrast I had gone to the human situation direct. Out of my own experience, observation, reading, and pondering, I had tried to face honestly and unflinchingly the world we actually live in, a world which provides fulfillment for millions but for other millions vast injustices, intricate tortures, irredeemable frustrations. This is not my speculation

99. See p. 5 in this book.
100. See Paul's concluding words in "A Masque of Mercy." Also, the poem, "The Fear of God."

but rather what anyone might see with his own eyes if he were not wearing tinted or distorting lenses. What comfort could there be in any God presiding over such a world? Better than such a God no God at all.

Unless, of course, my God were one of those metaphysical deities that can coexist with any amount of evil and injustice. Philosophers from Aristotle's day down to the present have often simply chosen some principle or factor grounded in actuality and called it God. John Dewey, to give a clear example, defines God as "the active relation between ideal and actual."[101] Such a God might be difficult to disprove, but could one reasonably and hopefully pray to him or it?

I too could pull such a metaphysical God out of my hat. But what good would it do me or anyone else? What could it do except to add further to theological confusion and buck-passing?

Frost never pried into my thought any more than I pried into his. There was plenty to talk about without reciprocal quizzing. At first I was too much in awe of him to be inquisitive, my whole effort being to take in what he said. And I assumed that a great poet would say something worth pondering whatever subject he touched on. I tried to discover Frost's religion from his poems, not from his conversation. It never struck me as strange that what he did say in the poems was so elusive.

101. *A Common Faith*, John Dewey (Yale University Press, 1934), p. 51. Dewey does not insist that this active relation between ideal and actual be called "God"; he insists only that this relation is indeed the reality behind the name and concept. He makes clear that he uses the word "God" to distinguish his position from what he calls "militant atheism," at the same time admitting that to use a word so steeped in the supernatural may cause confusion. On this point I differ with Dewey only in my conviction that it is more important today to avoid theological confusion than to find common cause with the supernatural religions. I am wholly in sympathy with Dewey's sharp distinction between the religious element in human experience on the one hand and particular religions and the generalized concept of "religion" on the other.

Gradually I came to suspect that what I was looking for did not exist, and that Frost had no consistent over-all philosophy. He picked up this or that shrewd insight or nuggety notion along the way, as a man might pick up a small curious stone to hold a while in his hand. To harmonize these insights seemingly did not greatly interest him. A profoundly thoughtful man, he was not a thinker. As far as his poetry is concerned it may have been well that he wasn't, for if he had worked out a comprehensive and cohesive pattern or system, his poems might have been prisoners within it.

Perhaps we do not insist that a thinker be wholly consistent, but I think we do require that he should at least recognize his inconsistencies. When Frost spoke at the University of Massachusetts in October, 1961, he began characteristically by offering some of his recent cogitations. There were two main points. (I condense and paraphrase.)

1. What is the most conservative thing in life? Inheritance, biological inheritance. What is the most radical thing? Our resistance to inheritance. All progress, all greatness, comes from our unwillingness merely to carry on the past.

2. America is hard to see, that is, the achievement and greatness of America; hard to see especially by us Americans. The Russians appreciate us better than we do ourselves, spurred as they are by fear and emulation.

Frost gave no hint of the lurking contradiction: namely, that the discontent of many Americans with the present state of their country may be one instance of the divine discontent he had been praising a moment before. If he had recognized the contradiction, he might have reconciled the two points of view by insisting that both were necessary for mutual correction and healthy balance.

On the question of consistency Frost could quote his master,

Emerson. "A foolish consistency is the hobgoblin of little minds."[102] Yes, dear Emerson, but when, precisely when, is consistency foolish and when is consistency not foolish?

With Thoreau, another master, the right to believe anything he wants to believe becomes positively rhapsodic, as a few *passim* quotations will show. "I do not love to entertain doubts and questions."[a] "I do not think much of the actual. It is something which we have long since done with."[b] "The truest account of heaven is the fairest and I will accept none which disappoints expectation."[c] "I fear only lest my expression may not be extravagant enough."[d] "The brave man never hearest the din of war, he is trustful and unsuspecting, so observant of the least trait of good or beautiful that, if you turn toward him the dark side of anything, he will still see only the bright."[e][103]

Compared to such wildness, Whitman, our third arch-optimist and defender of the inconsistent, gives a more persuasive statement.

> Do I contradict myself
> Very well then, I contradict myself.
> (I am large, I contain multitudes.)[104]

Though Frost is a far more sober and qualified optimist than his three great predecessors, he like them feels the need to defend his in-

102. From Emerson's essay, "Self-Reliance." The whole sentence reads: "A foolish consistency is the hobgoblin of little minds, adored by little statesmen and philosophers and divines." Then Emerson continues: "With consistency a great soul has simply nothing to do. He may as well concern himself with his shadow on the wall." Apparently it is not only a foolish consistency that is the hobgoblin of little minds, but any consistency at all.

103. These five quotations are from Thoreau's published *Journal*.

a) Vol. II, p. 46   d) Vol. VI, p. 100
b) Vol. II, p. 44   e) Vol. I, p. 97
c) Vol. III, p. 232

104. From "Song of Myself," Section 51.

consistencies. In the poem "To a Thinker" he compares thinking to walking: now right, now left. He concludes

> At least don't use your mind too hard—
> But trust my instinct—I'm a bard.

One may recall what he once said about the value of having two hands: so that we can hold opposites at the same time (entry for April 2, 1933). Frost is also quoted as having said to Sidney Cox many years ago, "It's well to have all kinds of feelings, for this is all kinds of a world."[105]

Frost's life, like his thought, was not composed and harmonious. There may be danger today of regarding the dark Frost as the true Frost and his benevolent aspect as only a Santa Claus mask. That this is not true the poems are abundant evidence. Everywhere you turn in them you find a sensitivity not only to nature but to human nature, a delicacy, an idealism. Especially you find these qualities in those conversations between husband and wife, "West-Running Brook," for instance, or "The Death of the Hired Man." Even in "Home Burial" where husband and wife are in conflict, the man who wrote the poem could understand and express the wife as well as the husband.

A full-length, book-length, portrait of Frost would be welcome today, giving us the whole man in all his diversity and inconsistency, and drawing upon all available studies, biographies, and partial portraits. The painstaking, devoted, and authoritative biography by Thompson could provide a sort of anatomical foundation for such a portrait. But though the portrait would not smooth over Frost's inconsistencies, it would emphasize his consistencies by discovering and developing themes running through his life. I should like to suggest

105. This statement may be found in two books: *Robert Frost, Original Ordinary Man*, Sidney Cox, p. 20; *Robert Frost, A Study in Sensibility and Good Sense*, Gorham B. Munson, p. 56. Munson quotes Cox to whom the statement was made by Frost; yet Munson's book was published in 1927, Cox's in 1929.

one such theme; and I can think of no other that touches his life and thought and art at so many points as does his *laissez-faire*, his inclination to let things take their course. In this he was perfectly consistent.

In the poems themselves there are people who illustrate this inclination vividly. There is the traveling agent for a country journal who not only illustrates the attitude in his life but puts it into words.

> And I lie back and ride. I take the reins
> Only when someone's coming, and the mare
> Stops when she likes: I tell her when to go.
>
> . . . . .
>
> I never dun.
> I'm there, and they can pay me if they like.
> I go nowhere on purpose: I happen by.[106]

Then there is the family of blueberry-pickers ("Blueberries") of whom someone says,

> Who cares what they say? It's a nice way to live,
> Just taking what Nature is willing to give,
> Not forcing her hand with harrow and plow.

Another figure is the gum-gatherer with his swinging bag of spruce gum and his easy down-hill stride.

Brown the farmer comes downhill more precipitously. Out doing chores on his hilltop farm one icy morning, he slipped and started sliding on the crust. As long as he resisted his descent he had a hard time of it. But when "he bowed with grace to natural law . . . he came down like a coasting child."[107]

Frost's formula for writing poetry we have already noted: "Like a piece of ice on a hot stove that rides on its own melting." Ideally a poem should almost write itself. And similarly in farming, cows

---

106. Lines from "A Hundred Collars."
107. The poem, "Brown's Descent."

should more or less milk themselves, and apples get picked spontaneously by natural law. If this *laissez-faire* strikes one as extreme, Frost can justify it theoretically, as in his poem, "Something for Hope." The argument runs thus: If your rocky pasture becomes overgrown with weeds, don't try to plow them out. Do nothing of the sort. Do nothing at all. Simply wait for trees to come in. After they are grown, cut them for lumber, and your land will be ready for grass again. A hundred years is provided for the full cycle. Any botanist or forester, I dare say, would vouch for the accuracy of the prediction. If waiting a hundred years for pasture improvement seems a long wait, be careful not to conclude that the poet is merely joking.

In another poem, "In Time of Cloudburst," the cycle is vastly longer. Instead of waiting a mere century for trees to grow, you wait a geological age for your eroded farm to sink out of sight and for a new farm of rich alluvial soil to rise from the sea. If you protest that this is too long a time, Frost might reply that this is what will actually happen, whether you wait or not.

Frost's God, as we have seen, does not meddle too much with man and prefers for man not to meddle too much with him. As in religion, so in politics and international relations: hands off, or if that is impossible, the light touch as on a steering wheel. Walls are good when they prevent too much meddling between neighbors or nations; but when they are no longer needed, walls themselves can be meddlesome.[108]

What shall we say of this attitude[109]—if we must say anything except that in Frost's own life it provided and protected a leisure (especially an inner leisure) for the poet's fulfillment? *Laissez-faire*

108. See "Mending Wall."
109. A fuller treatment of this aspect of Frost may be found in my essay, "Robert Frost from His Green Mountain," *Dalhousie Review* (Halifax), Summer, 1953.

in the saint is saintliness; in the lazy man, laziness. It would be hard to say just where Frost belongs between the two extremes.

> His head carved out of granite O
> His hair a wayward drift of snow
> He worshipped the great God of Flow
> By holding on and letting go.[110]

Someone might make a study of the gradual progress of Frost's reputation from the time of his return to America until his death. The earlier story is better known and more easily told: how he went to England in 1912, a very obscure poet, and returned three years later with two published volumes and the beginning of critical acclaim. But the story from then on is more complicated, for while his popularity with the common reader continued to spread, his standing with the literary elite lessened. How he finally won recognition from that elite and came to be included with Eliot, Pound, Yeats, Stevens, etc. as a poet for close reading, has yet to be told, so far as I know, in a complete study.

One turning point in Frost's favor was the publication in 1953 of two essays on Frost by Randall Jarrell in his volume, *Poetry and the Age*. Since the essays were influential, I should like to comment on them. Jarrell maintained that Frost was a great poet but that the great Frost was not the Frost that most readers knew and praised. However sound and important this view, Jarrell clouded his presentation by overstatement and a shrill hysterical tone. He kept swinging in opposite directions, now castigating those complacent readers who had embraced Frost for the wrong reasons and the wrong poems, now scolding the avant-garde for not embracing Frost for the right reasons and the right poems. The impression one got was that only Jarrell knew the truth. And Frost came to resemble the little girl who

110. Lines from "In Memoriam: Four Poets," in *Come Out Into the Sun: Poems New and Selected*.

had a little curl right down the middle of her forehead: When he is good he is very very good, and when he is bad he is horrid.

Now I must confess that this dichotomy strikes me as a dramatization and a distortion. To treat Frost's poems as sheep and goats, saved and damned, is as much an oversimplification as to regard them all as equally inspired or equally uninspired. The basis of Jarrell's judgment seemed to be the spiritual tone of a poem, not its effectiveness as a poem. Any hint of "hard complacency" means his rejection; while compassion or calm statement of fact, especially if dark and brooding, means inclusion.

But isn't dichotomy a crude sort of judgment, not much better than total acceptance or total rejection? The qualities we like in a poet and the qualities we dislike will usually be found in varying degrees and in various combinations. We can rate some poems as less successful or less agreeable or less significant than others without casting them into outer darkness.

As I go through the big volume of *The Complete Poems* once again, it becomes clear to me that I find the lyrics Frost's supreme achievement. In them Frost's wonderful warmth, playfulness, delicacy, wit, psychological insight, drama, and dark presentiment are caught in crystals of perfect form. It is the interplay, the mutual enhancement (and also the contrast) between the living substance of the lyrics and their classic exterior that give them perfection.

The same qualities, of course, are found in the longer blank-verse poems, the dialogues and eclogues; but there the vehicle is not perfect. Though Frost was a master of easy-going conversational blank verse and though a book could be filled with illustrations of his mastery, the problem of sustaining the underlying iambic beat and doing it without monotony was sometimes too much for him. He knew as well as anyone the need for constantly shifting the stresses in an iambic line for grace and expressiveness and flexibility; but in making these shifts to accommodate speech rhythms he not infrequently lost the iambic beat altogether; so that the line falls into a rocking rhythm with only four feet, and can be made to fit the iambic pattern only by forced reading. To illustrate this I quote the first five lines of "A Servant to Servants."

> I didn't make you know how glad I was
> To have you come and camp here on our land.
> I promised myself to get down some day
> And see the way you lived, but I don't know!
> With a housefull of hungry men to feed—

Read these lines aloud in a natural manner and you find the third line is not iambic at all but this: $\cup\,\underline{\perp}\mid\cup\,\cup\,\underline{\perp}\mid\cup\,\cup\,\underline{\perp}\mid\cup\,\underline{\perp}$. And the fifth line likewise collapses into this: $\cup\,\cup\,\underline{\perp}\mid\cup\,\cup\,\underline{\perp}\mid\cup\,\underline{\perp}\mid\cup\,\underline{\perp}$. The other three lines by contrast are too regular and plodding. Whoever reads by ear as well as by eye—and how else should poetry be read?—will be disturbed by this "crumbling" effect in many of the longer poems, and will also encounter many of the too regular plodding lines. Frost's fondness for monosyllables aggravates his problem, for it is polysyllables that most clearly establish and sustain a rhythm. It is likely, too, that Frost's custom of composing in a free flow prevented that rhythmic shaping and reshaping that the lyrics must have enjoyed.

This is not to say that these longer poems, in spite of flaws, are not great, some of them very great. I think first of the brilliant and sardonic "The Witch of Coös," and of perhaps the best-known of them all, "The Death of the Hired Man," the last seven lines of which are supremely masterful. Other favorites of mine are "The Ax Helve," "A Hundred Collars," and "The Black Cottage." Add to these some of the shorter blank-verse poems, "The Woodpile," "An Old Man's Winter night," "Mending Wall," "Directive," which in a sense mediate between the longer monologues and dialogues and the lyrics.

Still it is the lyrics I keep coming back to. If I could have the luxury of a volume of them for myself, I would certainly include the following, and others of course, for my list is not meant to be exclusive and final.

To the Thawing Wind
October
The Road Not Taken
The Oven Bird
Stopping by Woods on a Snowy Evening
To Earthward
Looking for a Sunset Bird in Winter
The Need of Being Versed in Country Things
Spring Pools
Tree at My Window
Acquainted With the Night
The Figure in the Doorway
Desert Places
Provide, Provide
Happiness Makes Up in Height for What it Lacks in Length
Come In
I Could Give All to Time
The Ingenuities of Debt
Choose Something Like a Star
Closed for Good

These are cut and shining gems. They burn with the singleness and purity of candles, but unlike candles they never burn out. Here, finally, are Frost's "momentary stays against confusion."

But now comes a last question. Why "momentary," Robert? Why aren't they permanent stays against confusion, enduring as long as the poems endure?

He might answer that they are effective stays only while in a reader's mind. But I would argue that even when a reader is not thinking of them consciously, they may still be in his mind, and of course he can always go back to them, again and again.

Frost might agree with me. Who knows?

In my autobiography I speak of having known three Frosts, and then, after his death, of finding a fourth.[111] It occurs to me only now that there was and is a fifth Frost whom I have long been reluctant to admit even to myself. This is the Frost I wanted Frost in his later years to be, and who seemingly could so easily have been.

The three Frosts I knew were such a rich experience that there seemed no room for any lack. With such richness why ask for more or different? So the fifth Frost hovered only as a beautiful ghost that I caught fleeting glimpses of. Now at last I want to confront that ghost.

Frost could have become my fifth Frost if he had been willing and able to forget his enemies, real or imagined, to take less seriously the expectations of his audience for entertainment, and to accept fully his great achievement and acclaim without the insatiable desire for more and more. If, standing on the platform of Johnson Chapel year after year, he could have forgotten himself and trusted his poems. If he could have read exquisite poems he never read, and made of them imaginative and artistic groupings. If he could have been willing to stop sparkling once in a while and merely glow.

If when consultant on poetry at the Library of Congress he could have sometimes foregone the pleasure of being cute. If when he went to Russia he had gone to make friends with the Russian poets and the Russian people, and not with delusions of political and diplomatic grandeur. And when he stood at the inauguration of John F. Kennedy if he could have been content to read the one poem he

---

111. The "first" Frost was the Frost in and behind the poems. The "second" was Frost on the platform. The "third" Frost was the man sitting face-to-face with me. The "fourth" Frost was the Frost of the letters to Louis Untermeyer. See *The Trouble With Francis*, pp. 86, 89.

---

started with. I could almost believe that the glare that prevented his reading the other poem was a divine admonition, and that the unmeddling God of Robert Frost was doing a little meddling. "Robert, you should never have tried to read *that* poem and never have written it."

May it be that Robert Frost, who had accepted his early bad luck with fairly good grace, was never quite able to accept his later good fortune?